Esla TEN
August 30th
Happy 202_
♡ Gramp_
Grandma M_

CREATIVE
ORIGAMI
AND BEYOND

Jenny Chan, Paul Frasco, Coco Sato, and Stacie Tamaki

Quarto is the authority on a wide range of topics.
Quarto educates, entertains, and enriches the lives of our readers—
enthusiasts and lovers of hands-on living.
www.quartoknows.com

© 2016 Quarto Publishing Group USA Inc.
Published by Walter Foster Publishing,
a division of Quarto Publishing Group USA Inc.
All rights reserved. Walter Foster is a registered trademark.

Art on front cover, back cover (top row), and pages 4, 5, and 58-97 © 2016 Coco Sato. Art on pages 6-57 © 2016 Jenny Chan.
Art on pages 98-113 © 2016 Stacie Tamaki. Art on pages 114-143 © Paul Frasco.
Photographs on page 116 (dollar bill) and art on page 119 (color wheel) © Shutterstock.
Photographs on front cover, back cover (top row), and pages 5, 58 (except for "Medallions"), and 59-97 by Barbora Cetlova of Barka Photography.
Photographs on back cover (bottom row) and pages 26, 27, 31, 37, 43, 51, 52, 57, 114, 115, 127 (bottom left), and 133 by Stephanie Carbajal.
Electro-origami projects on pages 76-97 completed in collaboration with Dr. Nicolas Seymour-Smith.
Text on pages 76-77 written by Dr. Nicolas Seymour-Smith.

Acquiring & Project Editor: Stephanie Carbajal
Page Layout: Erin Fahringer

All rights reserved. No part of this book may be reproduced in any form without written permission of the copyright owners.
All images in this book have been reproduced with the knowledge and prior consent of the artists concerned, and no responsibility
is accepted by producer, publisher, or printer for any infringement of copyright or otherwise, arising from the contents of this publication.
Every effort has been made to ensure that credits accurately comply with information supplied. We apologize for any inaccuracies
that may have occurred and will resolve inaccurate or missing information in a subsequent reprinting of the book.

6 Orchard Road, Suite 100
Lake Forest, CA 92630
quartoknows.com
Visit our blogs at quartoknows.com

This book has been produced to aid the aspiring artist. Reproduction of work for study or finished art is permissible.
Any art produced or photomechanically reproduced from this publication for commercial purposes is forbidden
without written consent from the publisher, Walter Foster Publishing.

Printed in China
3 5 7 9 10 8 6 4 2

MIX
Paper from
responsible sources
FSC® C016973

TABLE OF CONTENTS

INTRODUCTION

Origami is a centuries-old art form that has taken on new depth in today's art world, influencing trends in fashion, interior design, exhibition art, and more. *Creative Origami and Beyond* takes this traditional art form to new levels and guides you through a dynamic exploration of numerous ways to fold paper.

In the pages of this book, you'll find a variety of fun, easy-to-follow origami models across a range of styles, including traditional origami, miniature origami, wet-fold origami, and more. You'll learn how to create unique origami models, paint your own paper, and take origami to the next level to create wall art, jewelry, decorative objects, and more!

With the techniques and projects in this book—and helpful artist tips throughout—you'll soon be on your way to creating your own beautiful and unique origami pieces. So get ready—this is just the beginning!

HOW TO USE THIS BOOK

The projects in this book are designed to inspire you to create unique origami works of art, gifts, décor, and more! *Creative Origami and Beyond* is divided into four sections, each written by a talented origami artist with a unique twist on the art form.

There's no need to work through the projects in the order or section that they appear—choose the project that catches your attention first, and work your way through the rest as inspiration strikes. These projects are designed to engage and fuel your creative self. Allow your hands to lead as you fold your way through the projects in this book.

Ready to start folding? Turn the page to get started!

BASIC TOOLS & MATERIALS

he wonderful thing about origami is that paper can be found almost anywhere—it is affordable, portable, and it comes in a variety of shapes, sizes, colors, and textures.

Although traditionally executed with regular paper, you can create origami with just about anything pliable. Household items such as newspapers, magazine pages, wrapping paper, candy wrappers, dollar bills, and book pages can be folded to create one-of-a-kind, eco-friendly creations. You can even

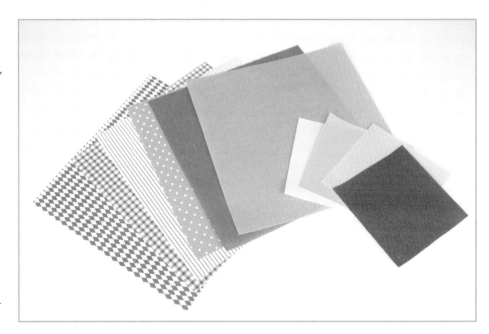

design and customize your own origami paper by covering plain surfaces with decorative washi tape, painting your own patterns, or printing favorite designs and patterns from your computer. Included in the back of this book are 8 sheets of origami paper to get you started.

PAPER & OTHER MATERIALS

If you prefer to purchase pre-cut paper, there is a variety of papers available online or at your local craft store. Machine-cut paper is convenient and ensures perfect squares every time. Economy packs are a great choice for the beginner folder. They come in a variety of shapes, patterns, and colors, and they are cost-effective—you can purchase them in packs of 100, or even 500.

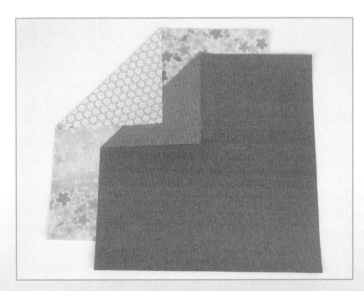

Large packs are ideal for practicing folds before using more expensive paper or moving on to more difficult models. Common sizes include 6" x 6" (15 cm x 15 cm) and 3" x 3" (approx. 7.6 cm x 7.6 cm), both of which are tangible sizes to work with. They are typically available single-sided (colored or patterned on one side, white on the other) or double-sided (different colors or patterns on each side). Sometimes, though less common, paper may be the same color on both sides. Choices are abundant and can include geometric shapes, gradients, animal patterns, flowers, and more.

Foil, hologram, and metallic papers can produce shimmery, eye-catching results. However, they can be more challenging to work with than economy paper. A beginner folder will benefit from practicing on economy paper first. Foil and metallic papers create permanent creases easily, are thinner, and typically curl at the edges. Foil paper also has less friction, resulting in a slippery surface that can be difficult to hold together. Like economy paper, metallic-coated and embossed-coated papers come in a variety of textures—some are made to resemble gold or silver sheets.

Handmade or washi papers are also good choices and are aesthetically pleasing. *Chiyogami*—washi papers with traditional Japanese patterns printed by either hand or machine—is usually more expensive, but is known for its high-quality and stunning patterns. *Momigami*, a kneaded paper known for its wrinkled look, is strong, flexible, and textured. Handmade paper can give finished models added depth, dimension, and overall elegance.

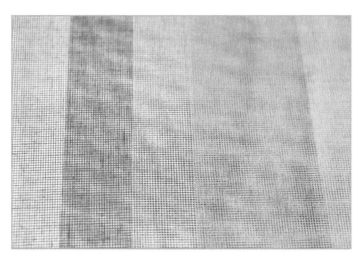

More unconventional materials to fold with include mesh, thin foam, or PVC-coated paper. Although sometimes harder to crease and hold shape, these materials are fun to experiment with and are typically sturdier, less subject to fading, and are weather-resistant and/or waterproof. All of these factors result in models that are perfect for long-lasting, outdoor displays. The transparency of mesh and PVC-coated paper also adds a unique dimension to the folds.

FOLDING TOOLS

Bone folders and paper scorers help create sharper, more accurate creases and reduce hand and finger fatigue. They are especially helpful when folding for long periods of time, working with thick paper, creating modular pieces (models that require more than one sheet of paper), or working with oversized paper. Traditionally made from bones of animals, such as deer, bone folders can also be made from wood, plastic, Teflon™, and other materials.

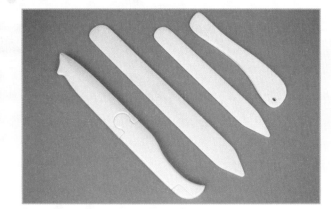

Bone folders come in a variety of shapes and sizes. Some combine multiple tools in one, like the one pictured below which has an embossing tip. Embossing tips are useful for getting into tight corners and for inserting paper into small areas where fingers cannot reach. The dull point prevents paper from tearing, making them better alternatives to sharper points. Alternatives to bone folders include the edge of your fingernail, a dull plastic knife, the side of a ballpoint pen, certain clay sculpting tools, or the edge of a ruler.

If you don't have a paper cutter, you can cut paper to size with a utility knife, straight edge (preferably a stainless steel ruler), and a cutting mat. Mark cutting points with a pencil.

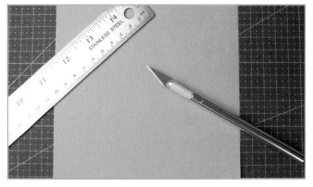

Traditionally, origami doesn't require scissors, but there are times when scissors are needed, such as when creating kirigami projects, which include a combination of folding and cutting. You can use standard scissors, paper crafting scissors, or precision scissors for smaller cuts. A large paper cutter is useful for trimming paper to size and cutting large quantities of paper.

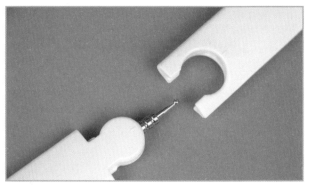

TIP

MINI WOODEN CLIPS HELP HOLD FOLDS IN PLACE WHILE YOU WORK ON OTHER AREAS. THEY ALSO HOLD PAPER TOGETHER WHILE GLUE DRIES.

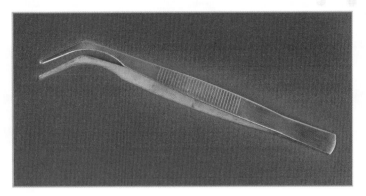

Flat, angled tweezers are helpful when maneuvering tiny folds or getting into difficult-to-reach areas. Tweezers with a PVC-coated surface work best, as the extra layer of PVC provides adequate grip, while the tool itself is non-marring and non-scratching.

STORAGE & DISPLAY

To prevent paper from wrinkling, use origami-specific storage that allows for easy access and storage of materials. Thin, plastic photo boxes are a good option for carrying paper and projects on the go.

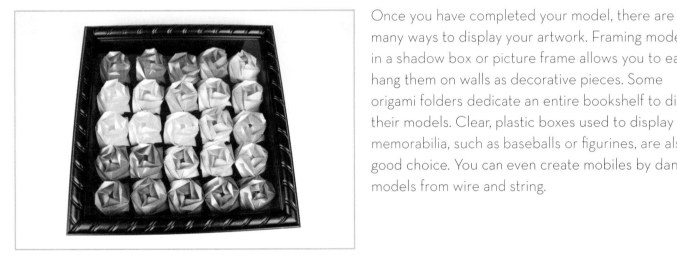

Once you have completed your model, there are many ways to display your artwork. Framing models in a shadow box or picture frame allows you to easily hang them on walls as decorative pieces. Some origami folders dedicate an entire bookshelf to display their models. Clear, plastic boxes used to display memorabilia, such as baseballs or figurines, are also a good choice. You can even create mobiles by dangling models from wire and string.

Three-dimensional origami roses displayed in a shadow box.

Additionally, two-dimensional models may be glued to greeting cards to create a unique, handmade gift.

BASIC ORIGAMI FOLDS

On the following pages are a variety of basic folds that will help you get started with origami. You'll find some of these folds in this book, and others farther along in your origami journey. These folds are all ideal for practicing folding. Observe the shapes created from the folds, and note how additional folds can drastically change the overall shape. Notice how the paper reacts and the direction it naturally wants to go. Practice identifying the folds by name as you encounter them in this book. With these basic folds, you can create boundless combinations and an infinite number of models!

The two most basic folds in origami are the valley fold (see page 11) and mountain fold (see page 12). You can differentiate the two by the way they look: One looks like a valley and sinks down; the other looks like a mountain and pops up.

The simplest way to illustrate these folds is by folding a sheet of paper in half. When creating the valley fold, the paper moves forward and over toward you. In contrast, when creating the mountain fold, the paper moves backwards and under and away from you.

FOLDING TIPS

- Fold on a flat, hard surface.
- Make sure your workstation is free from liquid.
- Align sides and corners before folding to create neater folds.
- Practice folds slowly.
- Fold firmly. Use a bone folder to help if you need it.
- Anticipate the final result before you finalize a fold.
- Work in a well-lit room—you need to be able to see what you're doing!
- Create a quiet environment where you can concentrate.
- Don't force any folds into place. If you need to force something in place, it means you're doing it wrong, and the paper will likely tear.
- If a piece of paper becomes too worn to fold, recycle it, and start with a new sheet. Worn paper cannot hold creases well and may crumble.

VALLEY FOLD

MOUNTAIN FOLD

VALLEY & MOUNTAIN FOLD SYMBOLS

Valley Fold Symbol

- - - - - - - - - - - - - - - -

Mountain Fold Symbol

- - · · - - · - - · · - - · - -

SQUASH FOLD

The squash fold involves prying open multiple layers of a sheet of paper, and then flattening to create a new shape. Here, two layers of a right triangle are pried apart and then flattened to create a square on the left side.

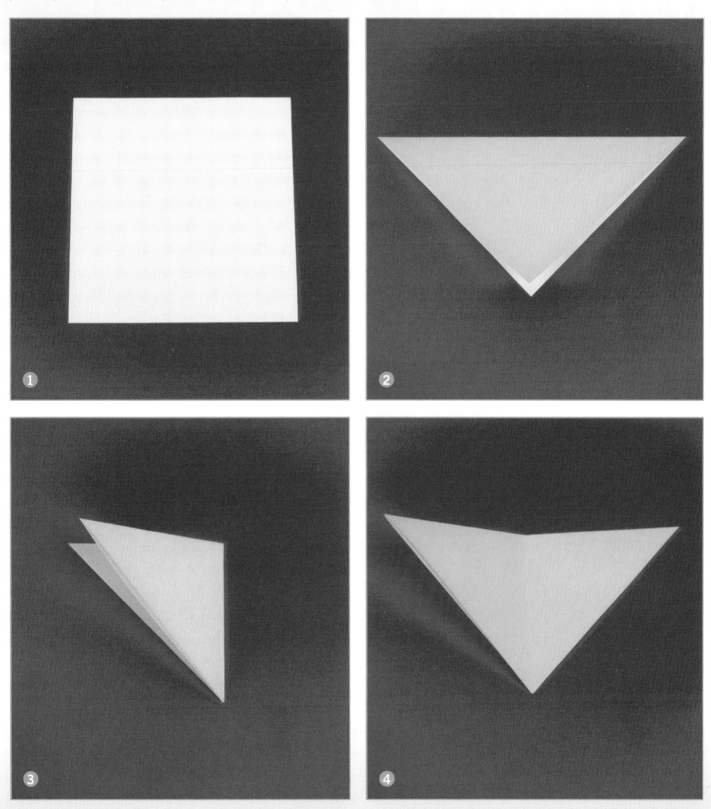

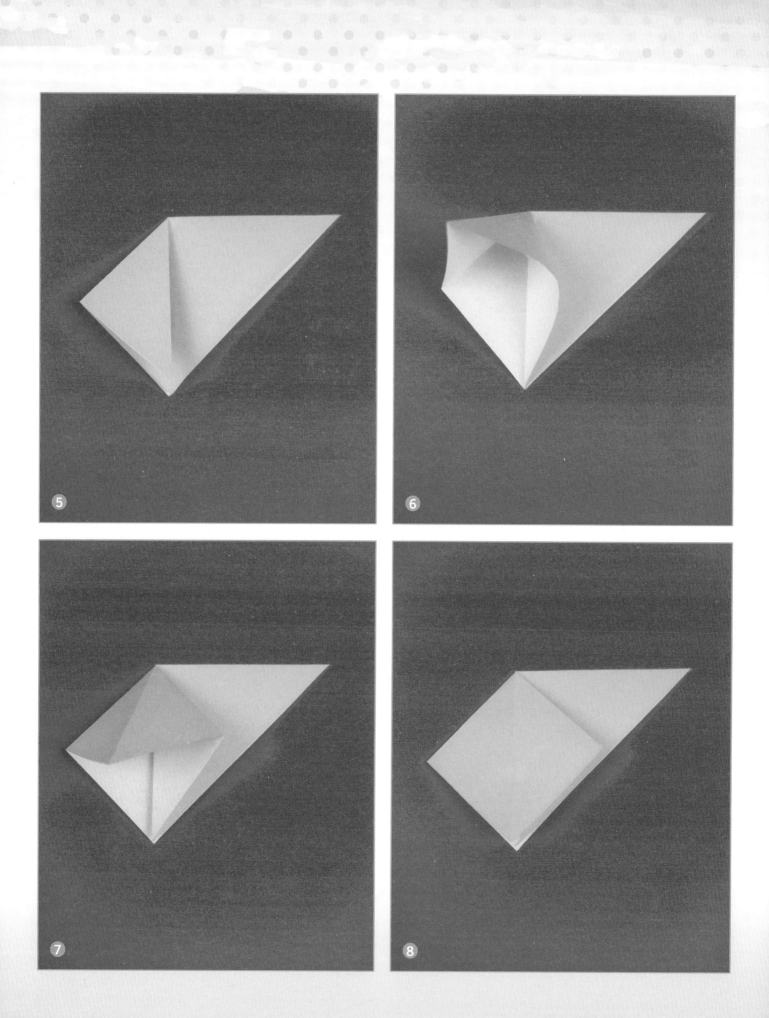

INSIDE-REVERSE FOLD

The inside-reverse fold involves: pre-creasing the paper at an angle, unfolding, reversing one of the outer creases and the center crease, and flattening from the side. The result looks like a bird's beak tucked inside the sheet of paper.

OUTSIDE-REVERSE FOLD

Think of the outside-reverse fold as the opposite of the inside-reverse fold. Similarly, it involves: pre-creasing the paper at an angle (in the opposite direction of the inside-reverse fold), unfolding, reversing one of the outer creases and the center crease, and flattening from the side. The result looks like a bird's beak placed outside the sheet of paper.

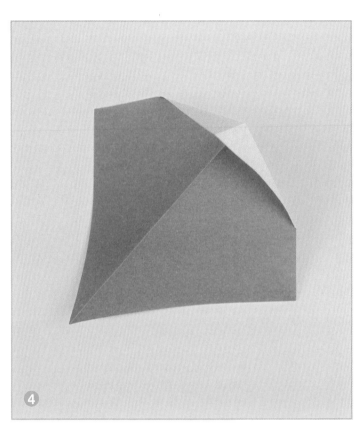

BASIC
ORIGAMI BASES

A great number of origami models start with a basic base. The following are a few of the most common bases used to create models. Like the basic folds, it's important to practice and understand these bases before moving on to more challenging models.

PRELIMINARY BASE

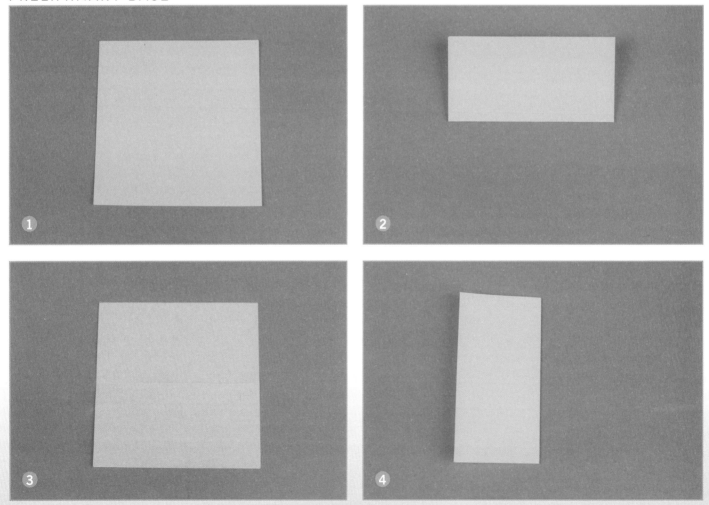

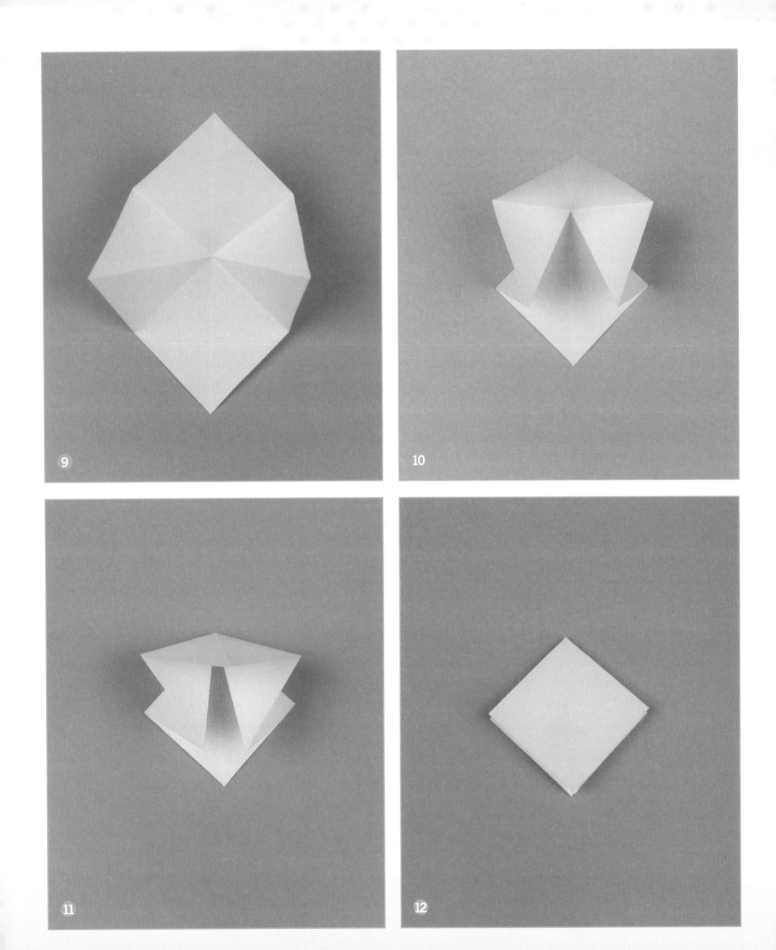

WATERBOMB BASE

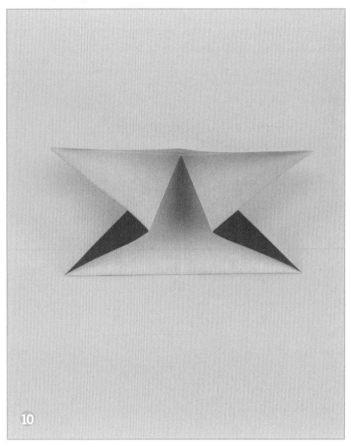

TIP

THE WATERBOMB BASE
IS SOMETIMES ALSO
REFERRED TO AS THE
BALLOON BASE.

KITE BASE

BLINTZ BASE

**BEAUTIFUL
ORIGAMI SWAN**

**FLORAL CORNER
BOOKMARK**

CREATIVE ORIGAMI

WITH JENNY CHAN

FOX ENVELOPES

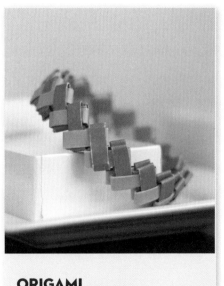

ORIGAMI CHAIN BRACELET

MINDFUL ORIGAMI

CREATIVE ORIGAMI
JENNY CHAN

BEAUTIFUL ORIGAMI SWAN

This graceful origami swan is a great starter project if you're new to the art of origami. Just follow the simple step-by-step instructions, and you'll have the hang of it in no time! All you need is one square sheet of paper. A 3" x 3" piece of paper that is pink on one side and white on the other will be used for this demonstration.

STEP ONE Start by folding the paper in half diagonally.

STEP TWO Unfold the paper, and then fold the top and bottom flaps to meet in the center crease.

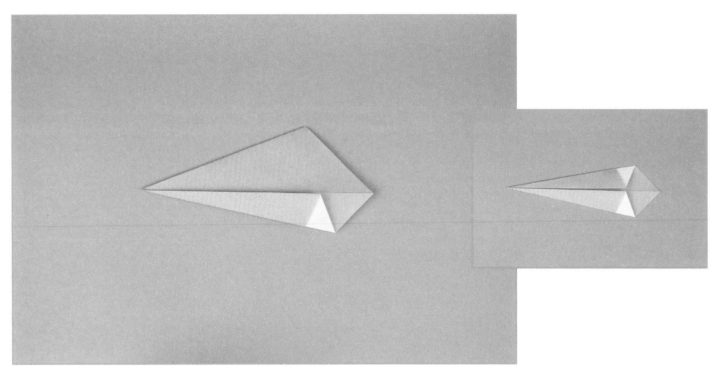

STEP THREE   Flip the paper over, and fold both the top and bottom flaps to the center crease.

STEP FOUR   Fold the left tip over to align with the right tip.

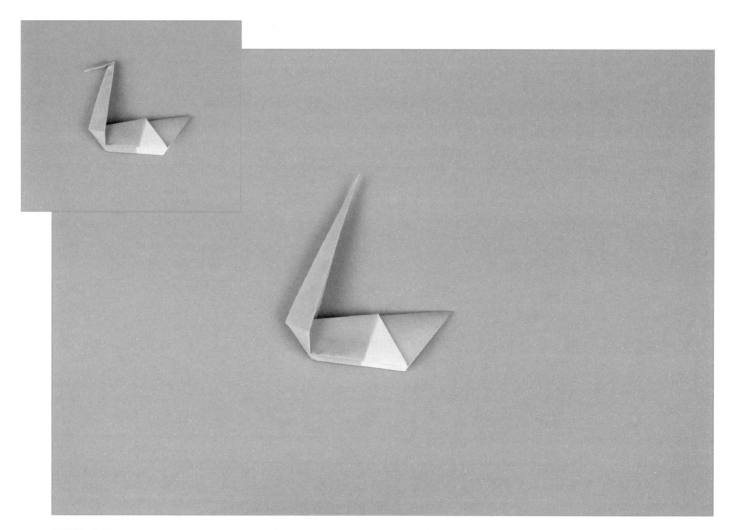

STEP SIX Angle the swan's neck by pulling upward and to the left simultaneously. Then fold and shape the head by folding at an angle.

FLORAL
CORNER BOOKMARK

DESIGN BY JENNY W. CHAN

Make a batch of these sweet floral bookmarks, and you'll never be caught looking for something to mark your place again!

STEP ONE   With the colored side of the paper facing up, fold in half lengthwise. Unfold, and repeat in the opposite direction. Unfolded, the paper should be divided into four equal parts by the fold lines.

STEP TWO   Next fold the paper in half diagonally. Then unfold, and repeat in the opposite direction so that the unfolded paper is divided into eight parts.

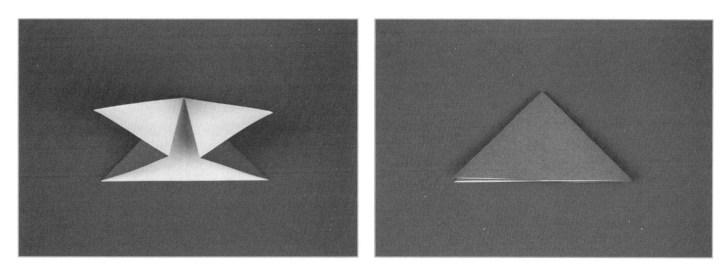

STEP THREE Using the creases you made in steps one and two, collapse the model to form the waterbomb base; then flatten.

STEP FOUR Fold the top right flap diagonally to the vertical center crease. Repeat on the left side.

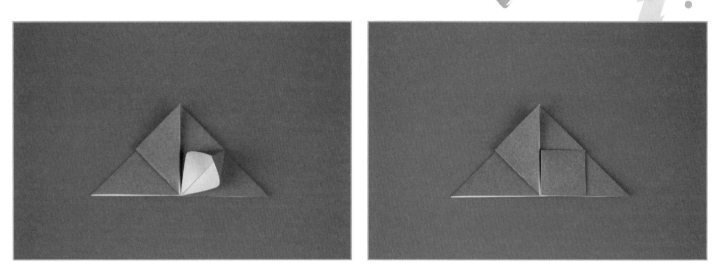

STEP FIVE   Slightly unfold the flaps you created in step four. Insert your finger into the opening and gently flatten to create a square (squash fold). Repeat on the other side.

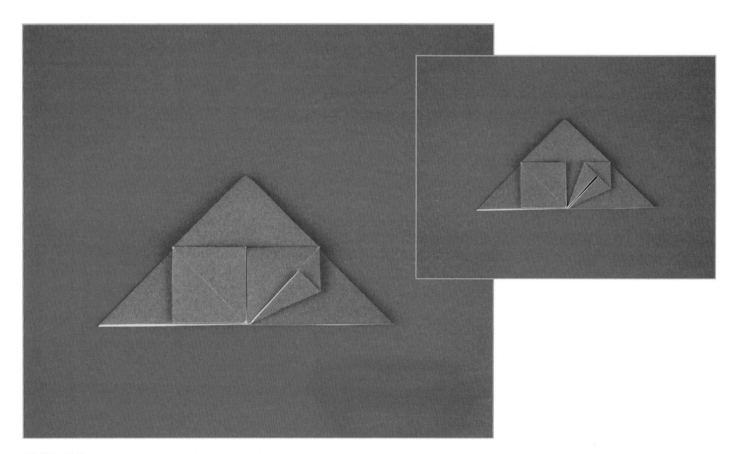

STEP SIX   On the right side of the model, fold the right flap diagonally to the center crease of the square created in step five. Repeat with the left flap.

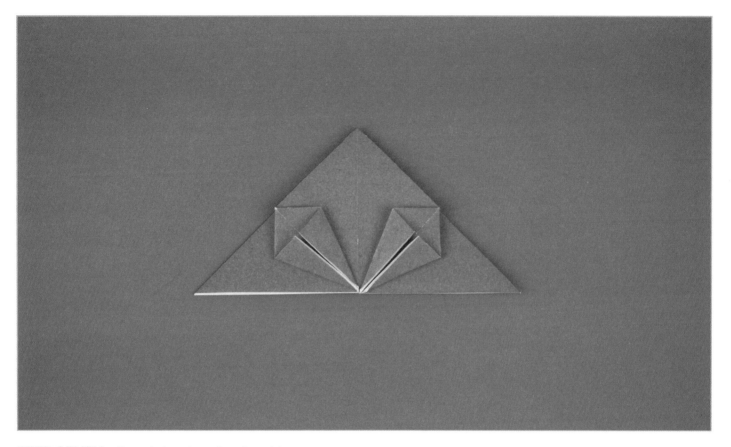

STEP SEVEN   Repeat step six on the other side.

STEP EIGHT   Slightly unfold the right-side flaps created in steps six and seven and insert a fingernail (or an embossing tip) into the opening and gently flatten to create a triangle.

Make a variety of bookmarks in an assortment of colors to brighten your favorite reads!

Two intersecting strips of washi tape take the place of ribbon in this classic gift look. Top with a bow cut from washi tape-covered card stock.

HAPPY BIRTH DAY
Helena

FOX ENVELOPES

DESIGN BY JENNY W. CHAN

These cute little envelopes will brighten up anyone's day—
better yet, they're a cinch to fold. Give it a try!

STEP ONE With
the color side facing
up, fold the paper in
half vertically.

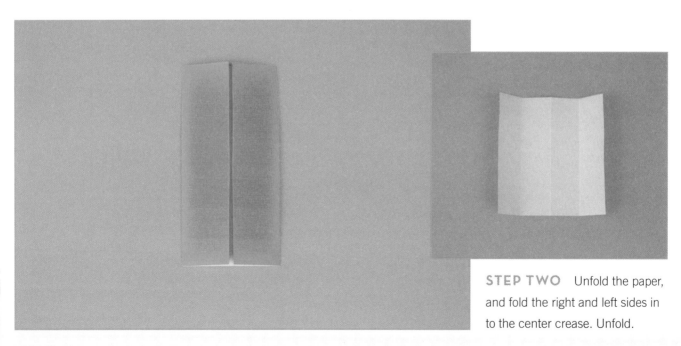

STEP TWO Unfold the paper,
and fold the right and left sides in
to the center crease. Unfold.

STEP THREE   Fold the right and left sides in to the outer crease that you created in step two. Unfold. There should be five creases total.

STEP FOUR   Next fold the top down one-third of the way.

Fold the right flap diagonally, aligning the center vertical crease with the top right corner. Repeat on the left flap.

STEP SIX   Align the right corner with the outer crease created in step three. Fold diagonally. Repeat on the left side.

Flip the paper over, and fold each of the top points diagonally to create the fox's ears.

STEP EIGHT Flip the paper back over. Fold the left and right sides along the outer creases that you created in step three.

STEP NINE   Fold the bottom up to the edges of the triangles you created in step six, and then unfold.

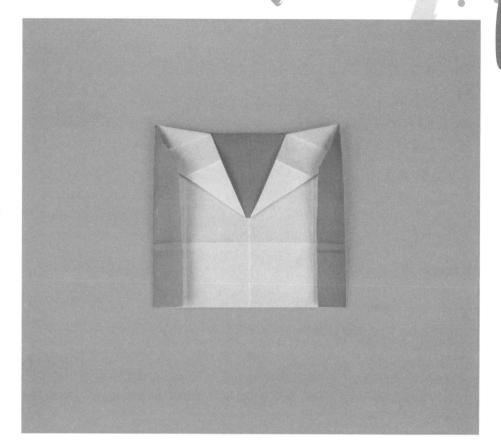

STEP TEN   Slip the bottom flap under the fox's nose, and add a black nose and eyes to finish!

ORIGAMI CHAIN BRACELET

This origami chain bracelet is an example of modular origami, which utilizes multiple sheets of paper to create the model.

MATERIALS
- Six sheets of 6" x 6" origami paper in two contrasting colors (e.g., 3 pink sheets and 3 purple sheets)
- Scissors

STEP ONE Divide each of the six 6" x 6" origami sheets into six 2" x 3" sheets. To do so, cut each sheet in half vertically, and then into thirds horizontally, as shown. After you've cut all 6" x 6" sheets, you will be left with thirty-six 2" x 3" sheets.

STEP TWO Fold one 2" x 3" sheet in half lengthwise.

STEP THREE   Unfold the paper, and fold the bottom and top sides to the horizontal crease.

STEP FOUR   Repeat step three to create a smaller rectangle.

STEP FIVE   Next fold the entire unit in half horizontally.

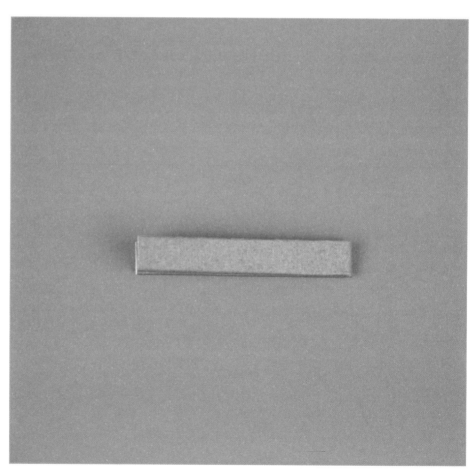

STEP SIX   Then fold in half vertically.

STEP SEVEN Unfold and fold the right and left sides to the vertical center crease.

STEP EIGHT Now fold the entire unit in half vertically.

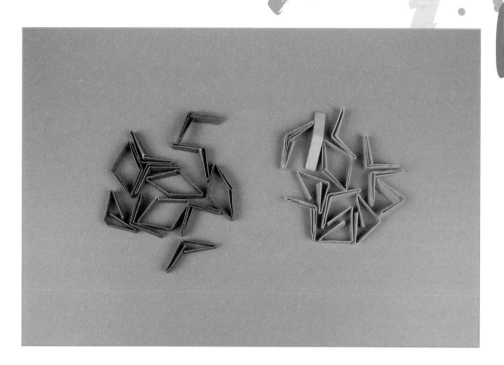

STEP NINE Repeat steps two through eight with the remaining 2" x 3" pieces of paper. You don't need to fold all 36 pieces, but you do need an even number (e.g. 32, 34, 36). For this bracelet, 32 pieces of paper were used to create a 3" diameter bracelet.

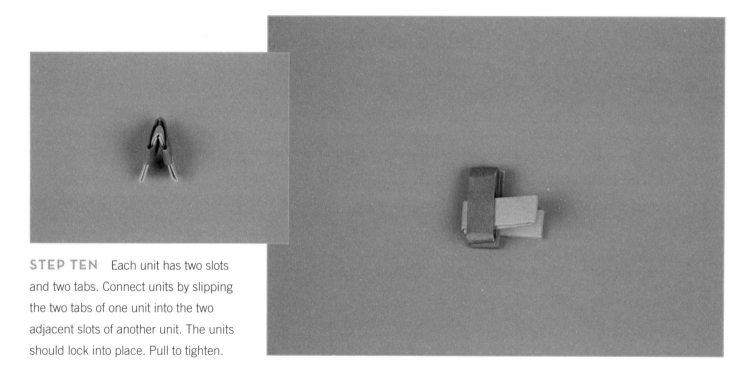

STEP TEN Each unit has two slots and two tabs. Connect units by slipping the two tabs of one unit into the two adjacent slots of another unit. The units should lock into place. Pull to tighten.

TIP
ADJUST THE BRACELET TO YOUR WRIST SIZE BY ADDING OR SUBTRACTING UNITS BY INCREMENTS OF TWO.

STEP ELEVEN Repeat step ten to continue adding units until the desired length is reached. You can alternate colors as you go, as shown, or you can randomize them.

STEP TWELVE To connect the ends, start by assembling the final piece as you normally would.

STEP THIRTEEN Unfold both tabs of the final unit. Here you can see the two tabs of the pink unit are unfolded.

STEP FOURTEEN Slip the unfolded tabs into the center opening of the adjacent unit. Here you can see how the two pink tabs are slipped into the center of the purple unit. Press the tabs in until they are snug, and you're done!

MINDFUL ORIGAMI: LUCKY ORIGAMI STARS

Technology has sped up our lives twofold. Days can turn to months and months to years without us even realizing it. It's incredibly important to take time in life to slow down, meditate, and reflect.

Folding origami allows your mind to focus on the task, and nothing else. The combination of creating art and using your hands has the ability to free the mind and relieve stress—whether it is related to relationships, health, finance, or something else altogether.

This lucky stars project is a great way to practice mindful origami because it is neither too easy nor too challenging—foregoing both boredom and frustration, respectively. Moreover, the final result is something that can be displayed proudly or gifted to someone who means a lot to you. The jar allows you to see your progress as your mind and body unwind.

Before you start folding, turn off your electronic devices and create an environment where you feel safe, comfortable, and relaxed. Put on some meditative music if that helps you to clear your mind. Don't worry about how accurate your folds are. As you practice you will improve, and folding will become second nature. Focus on how the paper feels in your hands and on how your hands become one with the paper. Ground yourself and concentrate only on the folding.

MATERIALS
- Paper strips (0.5" x 13.75")
- Jar (jars with a wide opening work best)
- Scissors (optional)

STEP ONE   Start with a strip of paper, white side facing up. Create a loop on the left end, and tuck it underneath the remainder of the strip.

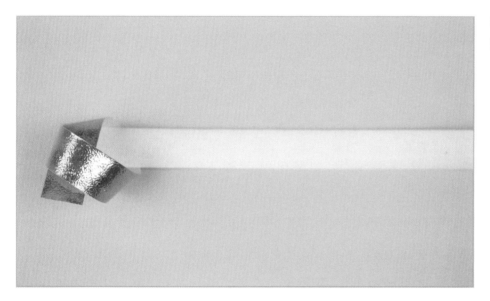

STEP TWO   Bring the shorter end through the opening, as if to tie a knot.

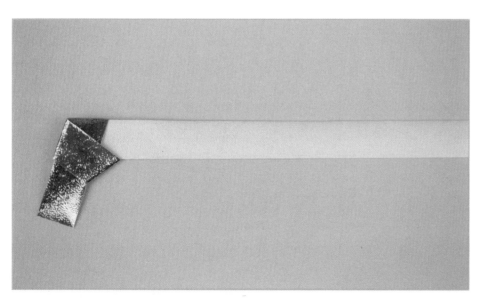

STEP THREE   Gently pull on the shorter end to tighten, and then flatten to create a pentagon shape.

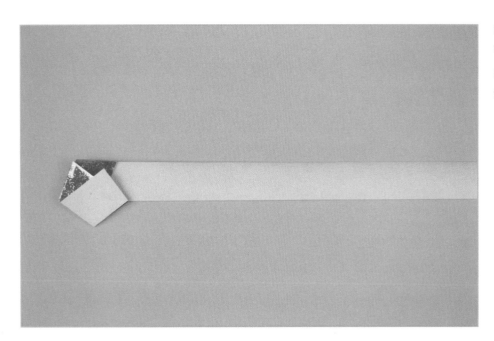

STEP FOUR

Wrap the short end around the edge of the pentagon.

STEP FIVE   Continue wrapping the pentagon along the strip of paper until you reach the end, while maintaining the pentagon shape. Refer to the four images below as a guide.

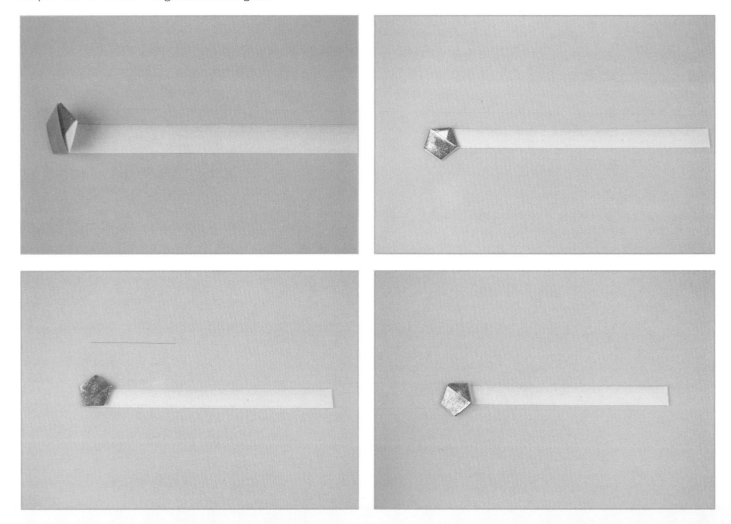

STEP SIX Once you've reached the end of the paper strip, it should look like this. If there is excess, trim it with a pair of scissors (or rip it with your fingers). If there is no excess, proceed to step seven.

STEP SEVEN Tuck the remainder of the strip into the nearest opened slot and flatten to complete the pentagon.

STEP EIGHT Carefully squeeze the top corner of the pentagon to form the first point of the star.

STEP NINE Repeat on each of the other points to complete the star and make it three-dimensional.

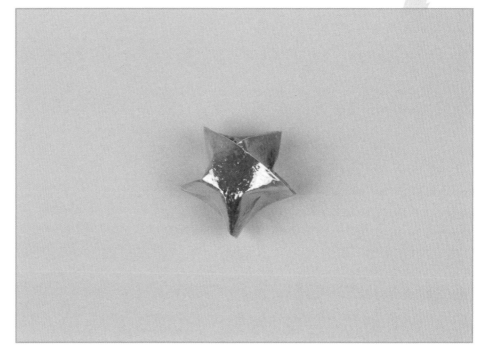

STEP TEN After completing your first star, relax, clear your mind, and make as many more stars as it takes to fill up your jar. You'll find that once you get in the flow of it, you don't need to think about the folding actions.

MEDALLIONS

BLOSSOM LIGHTS

LAMPSHADE

PLAYFUL, MODERN ORIGAMI

WITH COCO SATO

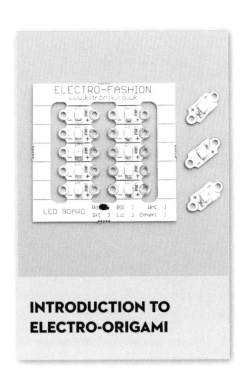

INTRODUCTION TO ELECTRO-ORIGAMI

LIGHTED ORIGAMI PURSE

FAIRY TIARA

PLAYFUL, MODERN ORIGAMI
COCO SATO

MEDALLIONS

DESIGN BY COCO SATO

Decorate your living areas or windows for parties with a gorgeous garland made of paper medallions. These are so easy to make and so pretty and versatile— you can create a garland, banner, wreath, or even a wall hanging!

MATERIALS

- Large paper (matte-surface gift wrap is ideal)
- Cutting mat
- Glue stick
- Hot glue gun & glue sticks
- Scalpel/craft knife
- Bone folder
- Metal ruler
- Pencil
- Scissors
- Twine & a twig/stick

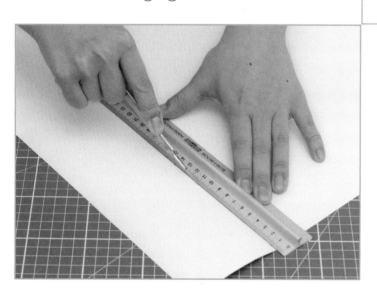

STEP ONE Measure, mark, and cut out strips of paper that are 24" long (60 cm) long and 3.5" wide (9 cm) with a craft knife.

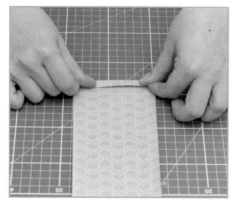

STEP TWO Accordion-fold a strip of paper, making the folds approximately 0.33" (1 cm) in size.

STEP THREE   To add snowflake-esque decorative details, mark and cut out small triangles as shown above.

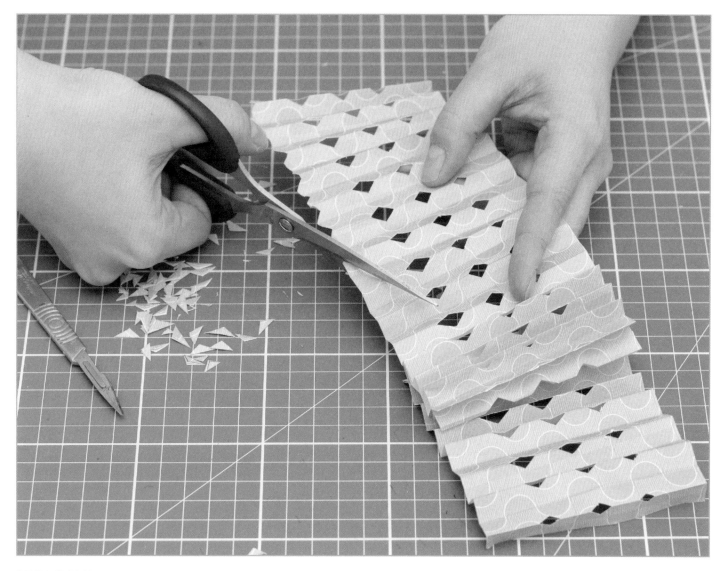

STEP FOUR   Use scissors to randomly cut along the long edge of the paper to create a frilled edge.

STEP FIVE Use a glue stick or double-sided adhesive to secure the ends of the paper together.

STEP SIX Turn the medallion over and push down in the center to lay flat. Then drop a large glob of hot glue in the center of the medallion. Hold the edges of the medallion to keep it flat until the hot glue is dry.

STEP SEVEN To hang, thread twine through one of the cutouts. Make several medallions to hang from your stick.

TIP

YOU CAN MAKE SMALLER MEDALLIONS BY CHANGING THE WIDTH OF THE STRIPS TO 2.75" (7 CM) OR 2" (5 CM). CREATE A VARIETY OF SIZES FOR VISUAL IMPACT.

BLOSSOM LIGHTS

Cherry blossoms are a symbol of spring in Japan. These flowers are delicate and have a very short lifespan, which may last a week—or just a blink. If a spring storm or rain causes the petals to fall, it's all over. This short, dramatic life, with the unpredictability and volatility of nature, and its delicate beauty influences the Japanese view of life. Make these blossom lights to decorate your space, and appreciate the beauty any time of the year.

MATERIALS

- 60 sheets of pale pink or cream 2.95" (7.5 cm) square origami paper (You can cut standard origami paper [5.9"/15 cm] into four parts.)
  Note: Five sheets of paper are needed to make one blossom.
- Cutting mat
- Bone folder
- Hot glue gun & glue sticks
- LED fairy lights (with small bulbs)
- Small clothespins or paper clips

STEP ONE   Place the paper color-side down, and fold it in half diagonally.

STEP TWO   Fold both sides to meet the center point.

STEP THREE   Place your index finger in the top side to open it up; then flatten it. Repeat on the other side.

STEP FOUR   Fold the top corner down so that it is flush with the edge. Repeat on the other side.

STEP FIVE   Fold the flap in half on the crease. Repeat on the other side.

STEP SIX   Squeeze a strip of hot glue down one of the flaps and press it to the other flap. Use a small clothespin or a paper clip to hold the flaps together for a few minutes until the hot glue is cool.

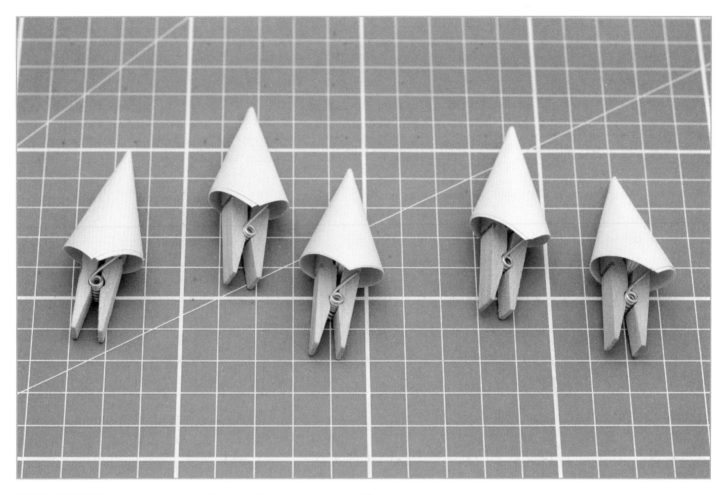

STEP SEVEN   Repeat steps one through six to create a total of five petals.

 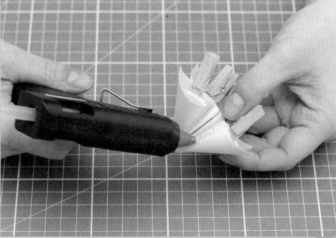

STEP EIGHT   Squeeze a strip of hot glue on the outside of one petal and adhere another petal to it. Hold the petals together with a clothespin or paper clip while you repeat the process, attaching three more petals.

STEP NINE   Before gluing the first and the fifth petals together to form a flower, insert an LED lightbulb in the center. Then glue the petals together.

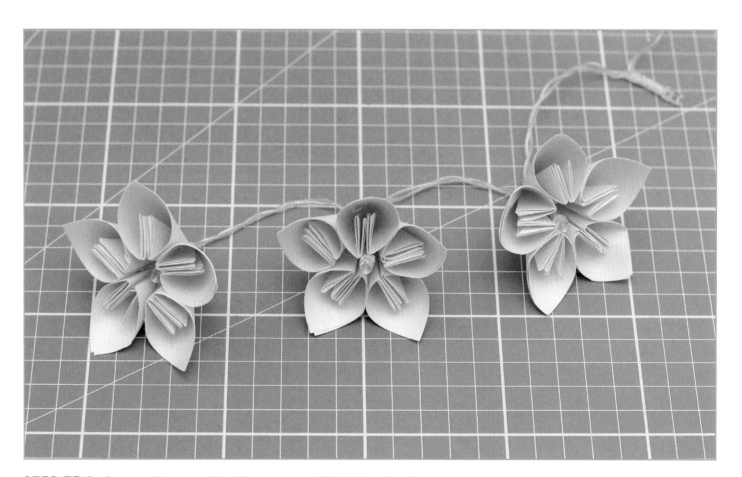

STEP TEN   Repeat all steps to add a blossom to each lightbulb on the strand.

TIP

THESE PRETTY BLOSSOM LIGHTS ARE PERFECT FOR YOUR MANTLE, ON TOP OF A BOOKCASE, OR ARTFULLY DRAPED ACROSS A WINDOWSILL.

PLAYFUL, MODERN ORIGAMI
COCO SATO

LAMPSHADE

DESIGN BY COCO SATO

Take your folding to the next level with a pendant lampshade with a simple, beautiful, and clean aesthetic. This white lampshade complements any interior and adds a stylish and modern touch to any room. With my detailed diagram, it's easy to make yourself—have fun!

MATERIALS

- 4 sheets of A3-size heavyweight (220gsm) cartridge paper
- Cutting mat
- Metal ruler
- Pencil
- Bone folder
- Scoring tool (see "DIY Scoring Tool" to make your own)
- Glue stick
- Cord or twine
- Single-hole punch

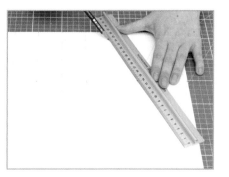
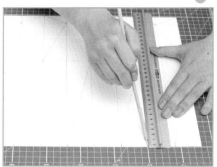

STEP ONE   Refer to the diagram on page 71, and mark each piece of paper with a pencil and ruler accordingly. Then score along the fold lines with your scoring tool and ruler.

DIY SCORING TOOL

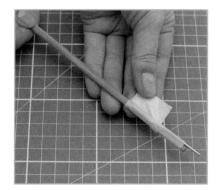
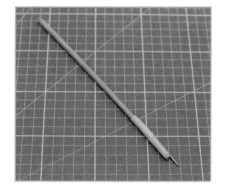

You can make your own scoring tool with a chopstick and an object with a blunt point, such as a knitting needle.

Simply attach the blunt point to the end of the chopstick with gaffer or duct tape.

Be sure to wrap the tape tightly and securely several times around the two pieces.

 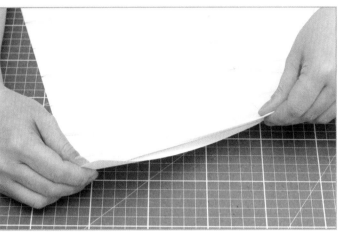

STEP TWO Carefully begin to accordion-fold along the lines one by one, referring to the diagram below.

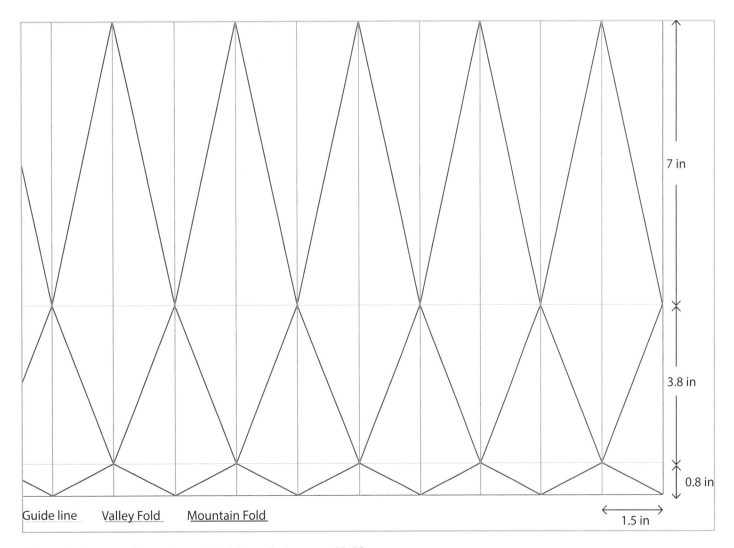

Guide line   Valley Fold   Mountain Fold

7 in

3.8 in

0.8 in

1.5 in

For a refresher on valley and mountain folds, refer to pages 11-12.

STEP THREE Continue folding the paper, following the guidelines in the diagram.

STEP FOUR Once folded, your piece of paper should look like this.

STEP FIVE   Repeat steps one through four three times to make a total of four folded sheets.

STEP SIX   Use a glue stick to join the four parts together at the edges, creating one long accordion strip.

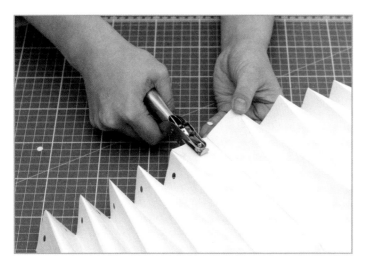 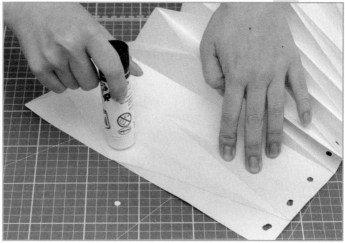

STEP SEVEN Punch holes along the top edge, as shown.

STEP EIGHT Glue the edges together to create a circle.

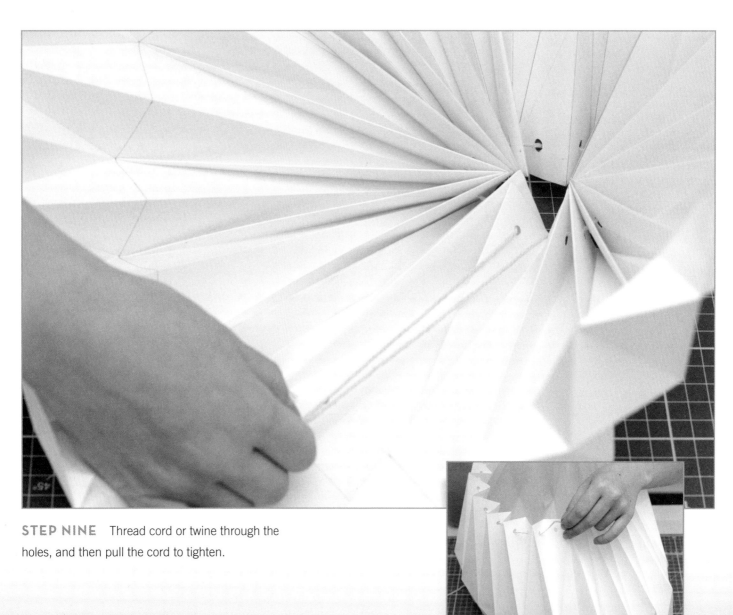

STEP NINE Thread cord or twine through the holes, and then pull the cord to tighten.

THE FINISHED SHADE IS PERFECT
FOR A HANGING LIGHT SWAG!

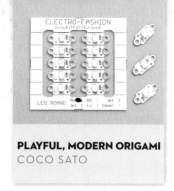

PLAYFUL, MODERN ORIGAMI
COCO SATO

INTRODUCTION TO ELECTRO-ORIGAMI

It might sound difficult, but it only takes a few simple, affordable, easy-to-find tools to turn plain paper models into brilliant, lighted statement pieces!

The guides in this section will tell you everything you need to know to make a finished electro-origami piece. If you want to learn more, you can go to Adafruit's brilliant learning site (www.learn.adafruit.com) for extra tips and guides. All the components used here are available affordably from many online stores, including www.adafruit.com in the US, and www.maplin.co.uk in the UK.

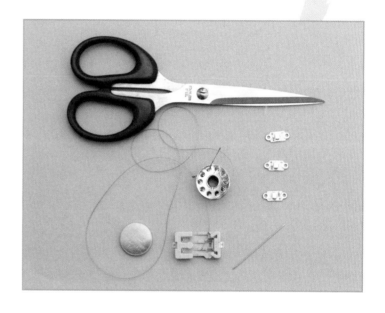

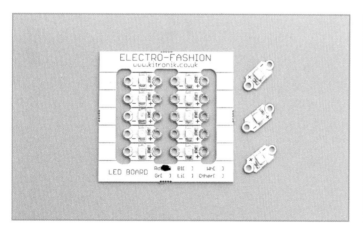

SEWABLE LED SEQUINS   Also known simply as "sewable LEDs," these tiny electric lights are bright, simple to use, and come in a range of beautiful colors. When connected to batteries using electrically conductive thread they can stay lit for hours, or even days.

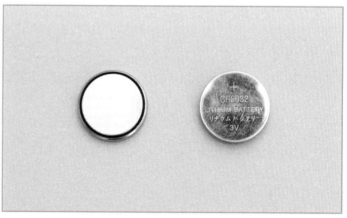

COIN CELL BATTERY   These batteries provide power for the LED sequins. Note that one side of these batteries—the shiny side—is marked with a large plus sign "+". These batteries are available at many convenience and electronics stores. Be careful to only buy those labeled as "CR2032." This is the most common type, and other types might not fit in the battery holder.

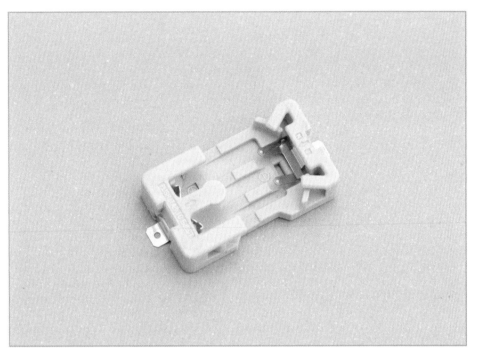

COIN CELL BATTERY HOLDER

The battery holder (also known as a battery clip) provides a convenient way to sew the battery into the project and connect it to the LED sequins. These holders also have metal hoops on opposite sides, which are used to fasten conductive thread. The holder is marked with a small minus sign "-" closer to one of the sides. It can sometimes be difficult to read, so when you've found it you can use a permanent marker to make a more obvious mark on the plastic! When purchasing the holder, make sure it fits the most common type of coin cell battery, the "CR2032."

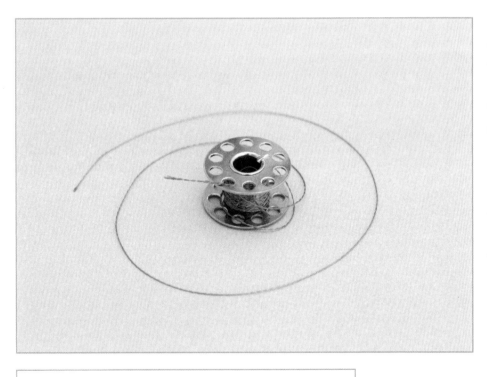

CONDUCTIVE THREAD

Conductive thread is special thread made from a mixture of common thread and metal strands. It is reasonably soft and flexible for sewing, but also conducts electricity like a wire. This thread will be used to connect the battery holder and LED sequins and complete the shining light circuits. Although it is soft enough to sew into most projects, the metal also makes it a bit more "springy" than normal thread—it can take some getting used to.

ADDITIONAL TOOLS & MATERIALS

In addition to the electronic components listed above, it's also helpful to have a couple of extra tools on hand:

- Sharp scissors
- A sturdy needle
- Hot glue gun & glue sticks

LIGHTED ORIGAMI PURSE

When going out, I always want to be prepared, so I keep essential items such as bandages, lip balm, bobby pins, and chewing gum in a small purse. This absolutely charming expandable purse is perfect for carrying small items to any party in style. By following this tutorial, you will have a special, one-of-a-kind purse that lights up! Each accordion fold gives this purse its expandability, allowing you to fit bulkier items in too.

The finished purse measures 6.3" x 3.4" (16 cm x 8.5 cm).

MATERIALS

- A piece printer paper (140gsm), A3 (16.5" x 11.7" /42 cm x 29.7 cm/) or 11.8" x 11.8" (30 cm x 30 cm), for purse insert (See "Making a Square from a Rectangular Sheet of Paper.)
- A piece of heavyweight paper (220gsm), A4 (12" x 8.3"/29.7 cm x 21 cm) for purse cover base
- A piece of patterned paper or fabric, A4 (or larger than 18" x 7"/28 cm x 18 cm)
- Ribbon (25"/65cm)
- Cutting mat
- Metal ruler
- Pencil
- Folding bone
- Scoring tool (See page 70 to make your own.)
- Glue stick
- Sharp scissors
- Hot glue gun & glue sticks
- Masking tape
- Scalpel/craft knife
- 2 LED sequins
- Coin cell battery
- Coin cell battery holder
- Conductive thread
- A sturdy needle

PURSE INTERIOR

STEP ONE   Place the square piece of paper on the mat. Fold and unfold diagonally in both directions.

MAKING A SQUARE FROM A RECTANGULAR PIECE OF PAPER

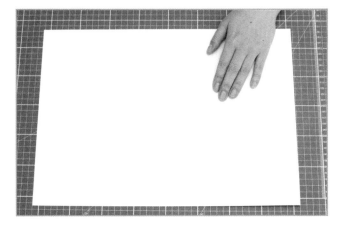

Lay a rectangular sheet of paper horizontally, as shown.

Fold one corner of the paper until it meets the opposite edge, forming a triangle; then crease with a bone folder.

Cut the excess paper.

Unfold.

STEP TWO   Next fold and unfold lengthwise and widthwise.

STEP THREE   Fold the outside edges to meet at the central crease.

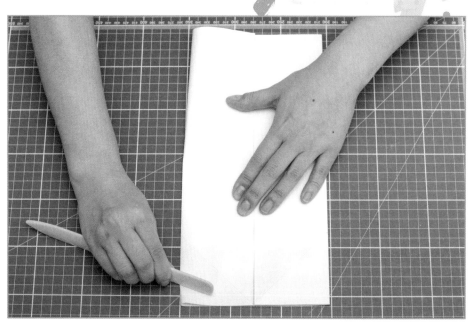

STEP FOUR

Unfold and fold the other side edges to meet at the center crease.

STEP FIVE

Mountain-fold the center crease to form a peak, using the creases you have made as shown.

STEP SIX Push the peak to one side.

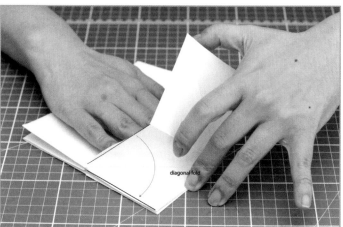

STEP SEVEN Open up the top layer, and make a crease that runs diagonally from the edge of the top layer to the central point, as shown here.

STEP EIGHT
Crease well, and then repeat on the other side.

STEP NINE
Push the corners inward.

STEP TEN   Press the folds firmly.

STEP ELEVEN   Turn over, and repeat steps seven to ten.

STEP TWELVE
Glue down the corner triangle flaps at each end—now you have completed the expandable purse insert.

PURSE COVER
(DESIGN BY COCO SATO)

The cover is made from one piece of heavyweight paper and an outer layer of patterned or luxuriously textured paper or fabric of your choice. The outer layer will measure an extra 0.3"-0.4" around in size.

STEP ONE   For the base of the cover, cut a sheet of heavyweight printer paper into a rectangle measuring 10.2" x 6.3" (26 cm x 16 cm). Use a pencil to mark where you will create score lines, referring to the "Purse Cover Base Diagram" on page 83. Then score the paper.

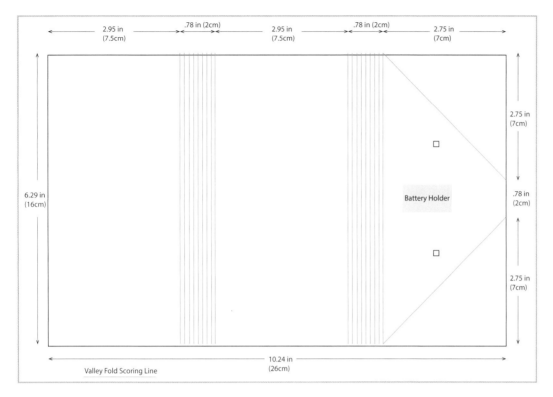

| 2.95 in (7.5cm) | .78 in (2cm) | 2.95 in (7.5cm) | .78 in (2cm) | 2.75 in (7cm) |

6.29 in (16cm)

2.75 in (7cm)

Battery Holder

.78 in (2cm)

2.75 in (7cm)

10.24 in (26cm)

Valley Fold Scoring Line

Purse Cover Base Diagram

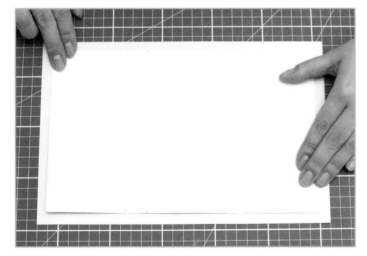

STEP TWO   Place the patterned paper or a piece of fabric of your choice for the cover on the mat, and trim it to 18" x 7" (28 cm x 18 cm). The outer cover paper or fabric should be about 0.4" (1 cm) larger than the cover base on all four sides.

STEP THREE   Use a glue stick to liberally apply glue to the back of the cover base, and center it on the outer cover. Press down firmly to adhere, and allow the glue to dry for about 10 minutes. Then score around the edges where the cover base and outer cover meet.

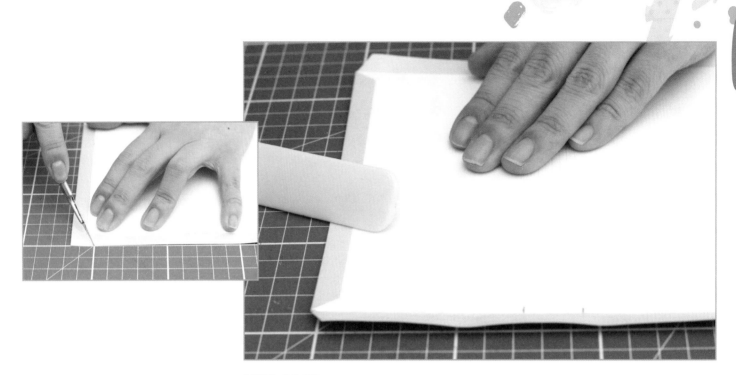

STEP FOUR Cut the corners of the outer cover, as shown in the inset. Then apply glue neatly to the edges. Fold the edges of the outer cover over the cover base. Press the edges down with the folding bone for a neat finish.

STEP FIVE Mark two 0.1" x 0.1" (3mm x 3mm) squares where the LED sequin lights will be placed. Then cut the squares out using a sharp scalpel. The purse cover is now ready for adding the LED sequins.

ELECTRONICS

The next few steps demonstrate how to make the complete circuit. Please note: Do NOT insert the battery into the holder until step seven, for testing. After testing, remove the battery again until you complete the project!

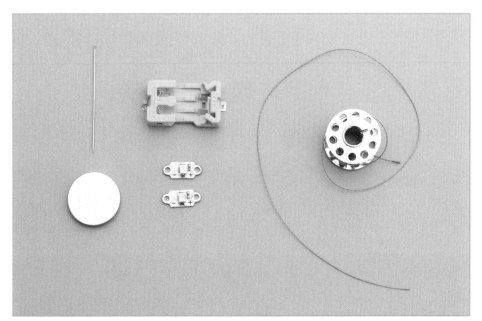

STEP ONE
Gather two LED sequins, a coin cell battery, a coin cell battery holder, conductive thread, and a sturdy needle.

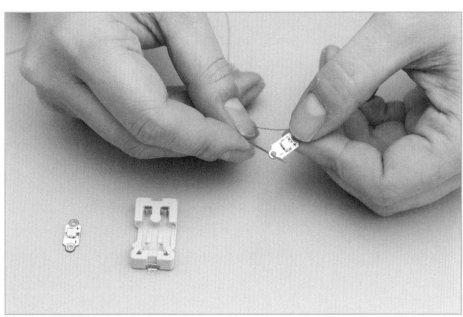

STEP TWO   Thread the needle with at least 12" (30 cm) of conductive thread. Use the needle to guide the thread through the first sequin on the side marked with a minus sign "-". Loop it around a couple of times, and tie a sturdy knot. It's important that the knots are tight around the metal hoops to ensure a good connection.

STEP THREE Guide the remainder of the thread through the metal hoop on the battery holder on the side marked with a minus sign "-". Loop it around a couple of times, and tie a sturdy knot so that the thread is fastened tightly to the holder, leaving about 1" (3 cm) of thread between the holder and the first sequin.

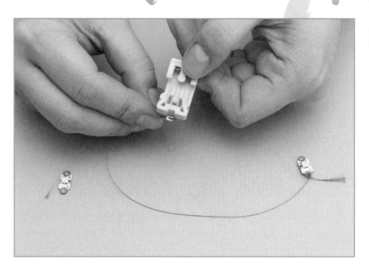

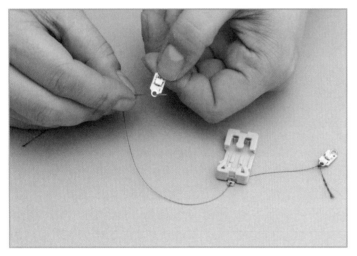

STEP FOUR Thread the second sequin on the side marked with a minus sign "-". Loop it around a couple of times, and tie a sturdy knot so that the thread is fastened tightly to the holder. Leave about 1" (3 cm) of thread between the holder and the second sequin.

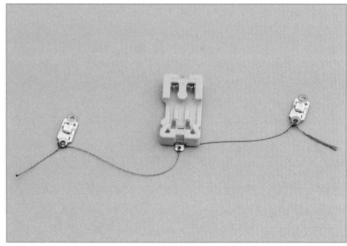

STEP FIVE Cut off any loose thread. The completed minus sign "-" side will look like this.

STEP SIX Repeat steps two through five on the plus sign "+" side to complete both circuits.

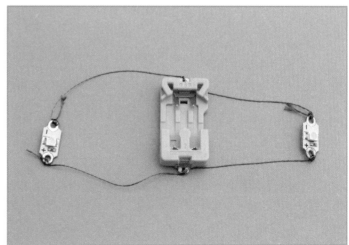

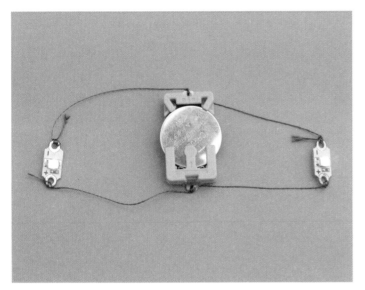

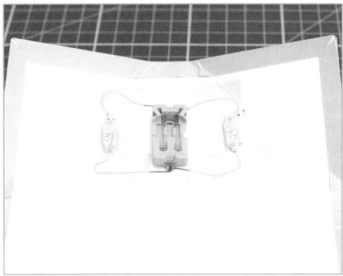

STEP SEVEN   Before adding the circuit to the origami, test it! I recommend taping down any leftover loose ends and thread (not shown in the photograph). It's very important that the threads do not cross over or touch one another! Insert the battery, plus sign "+" facing up. The LED sequins should light up! Remove the battery before you move on to the next steps. You will put it back in at the end.

STEP EIGHT   Place the circuit on the origami, with the LED sequin lights poking through the holes on the front face. Use masking tape to tape down any slack thread, ensuring that no thread overlaps or touches any other—take special care where the folds are. You can insert the battery to make sure the sequins still work, but be sure to take it out again.

STEP NINE   Put a drop of hot glue behind the battery holder and press down firmly in place.

STEP TEN   Fold over the triangular corners to hide the circuits, and glue them down. Rub with a folding bone, pressing firmly to secure.

STEP ELEVEN Apply glue liberally to one of the outer sides of the purse insert. Then place the glued side of the insert on the cover, with the accordion opening facing toward the purse cover flap. The insert should fit within the scored lines.

STEP TWELVE

Apply glue liberally to the other outer side of the purse insert, and then glue to the cover. The purse insert should fit neatly within the cover as shown.

STEP THIRTEEN

Complete by adding a ribbon for tying the purse closed. Apply a drop of hot glue just above the battery holder on the cover, and glue the ribbon down. Add the battery, and you're ready for a night out on the town!

FAIRY TIARA

DESIGN BY COCO SATO

Who doesn't like to feel special at a party? Make this elegant yet playful modular origami tiara for birthdays, celebrations, or summer festivals. Decorated with sparkly LED lights, it's sure to make anyone feel like a king or queen for the day!

MATERIALS

- A piece of printer paper (140gsm), A3 (16.5" x 11.7"/42 cm x 29.7 cm)
- Ribbon (60"/150cm)
- Cutting mat to protect your work surface
- Metal ruler
- Pencil
- Folding bone
- Scoring tool (See page 70 to make your own.)

- Glue stick
- Stapler
- Masking tape
- Scalpel/craft knife
- Sharp scissors
- 3 LED sequins
- Coin cell battery
- Coin cell battery holder
- Conductive thread
- A sturdy needle

STEP ONE

Lay a sheet of A3 paper horizontally, as shown, and mark where to cut by referring to the diagram on page 91.

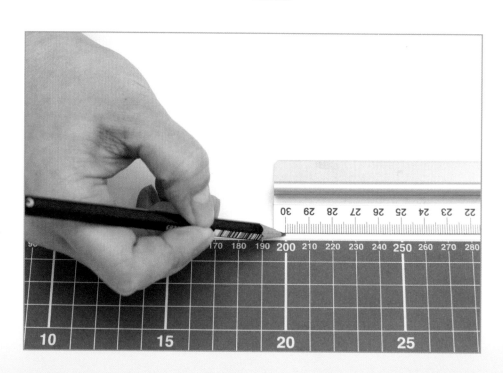

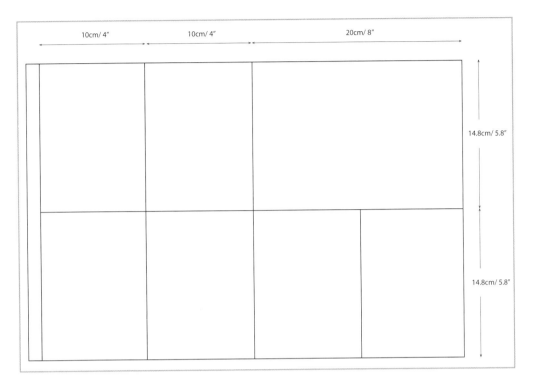

Tiara Cut Diagram

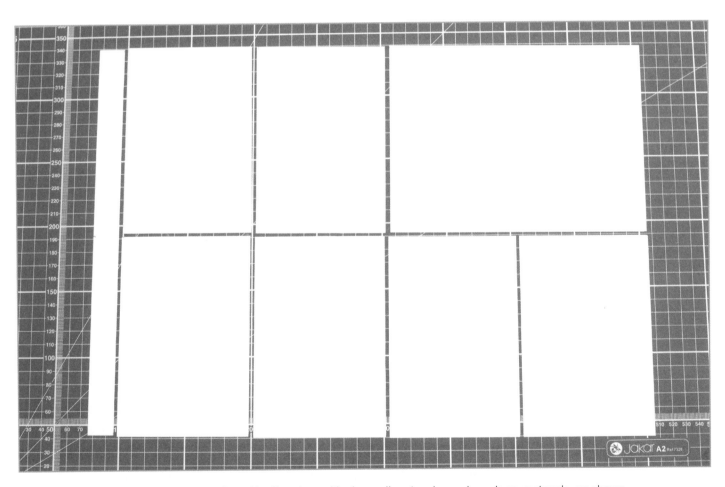

STEP TWO Cut the paper into sections. You'll end up with six small rectangles and one large rectangle, as shown.

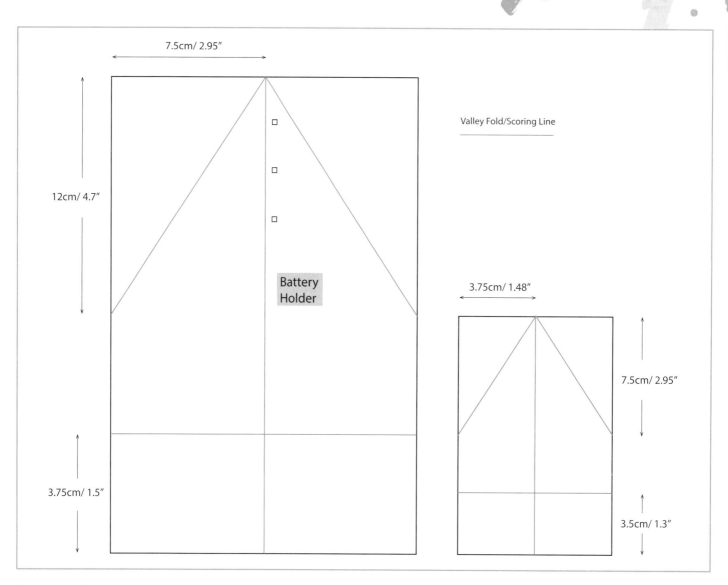

7.5cm/ 2.95"

12cm/ 4.7"

Valley Fold/Scoring Line

Battery Holder

3.75cm/ 1.5"

3.75cm/ 1.48"

7.5cm/ 2.95"

3.5cm/ 1.3"

Tiara Score Diagram

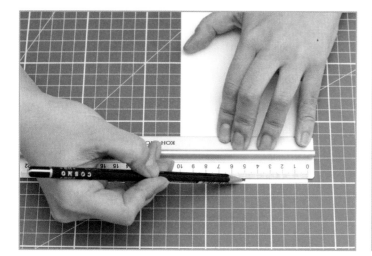

STEP THREE   Refer to the score diagram above to make guide marks with a pencil.

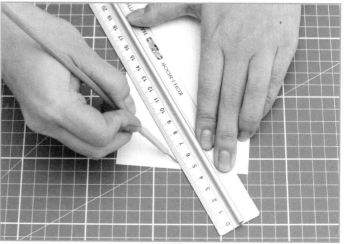

STEP FOUR   Score each of the six small rectangles and the large rectangle, as shown.

STEP FIVE
Fold each piece
of paper firmly.

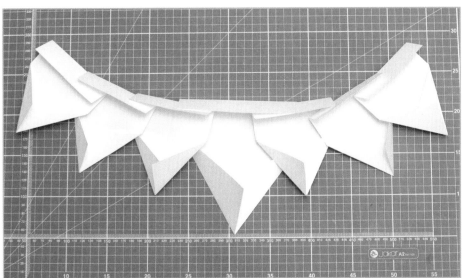

STEP SIX
When each
piece is folded,
they should look
like this.

STEP SEVEN   Take the six small pieces, and glue the
corners together at the point. Set aside the large one for now—
the lights and batteries will be attached to that piece later.

STEP EIGHT   Cut a 60" (150cm) ribbon in half. Use a
stapler to attach one piece of ribbon securely to one of the small
origami pieces. Repeat the process to attach the second piece of
ribbon to another of the small origami pieces.

The next few steps will guide you in making the complete circuit shown at below left. Please note: Do NOT insert the battery into the holder until step four for testing. After testing, remove the battery again until you complete the project!

ELECTRONICS

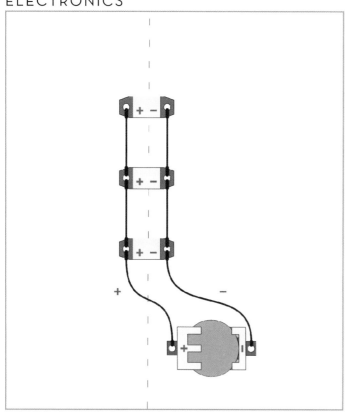

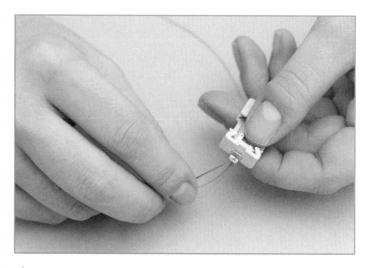

STEP ONE   Thread a sturdy needle with at least 16" (40 cm) of conductive thread. Use the needle to guide the thread through the metal hoop on the battery holder on the side marked with a minus sign "-". Loop it around a couple of times, and tie a sturdy knot so that the thread is fastened tightly to the holder. It's important for the knots to be tight around the hoops in order to have a good connection.

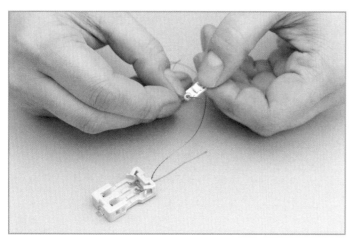

STEP TWO   Thread the rest of the thread through the first sequin on the side marked with a minus sign "-". Loop it around the sequin's hoop and tie sturdy knot. Leave about 0.75" (2 cm) of thread between the holder and the sequin.

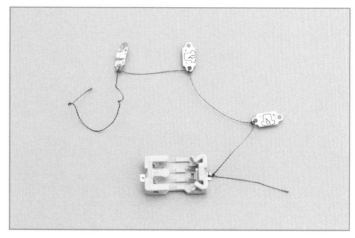

STEP THREE   Thread the same thread through the second and third sequins on the sides marked with a minus sign "-", making sure to tie them off tightly. Leave about 1"-1.5" (3-4 cm) between the sequins.

STEP FOUR   Repeat steps one through three on the plus sign "+" side to complete both circuits, and cut off any loose thread. Before adding the circuit to the origami piece, test it. Tape down any leftover loose ends and thread—remember that it's important that the threads do not cross over or touch one another! Insert the battery, with the plus sign "+" facing up. The LED sequins should light up! Remove the battery before moving on to the next steps.

STEP FIVE   Place the large origami piece down with the backside up. Mark 0.1" x 0.1" (3 x 3mm) squares just beside the center crease line. These mark where the LED lights will poke through. Cut the squares out with a craft knife.

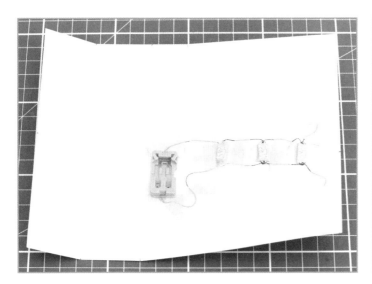

STEP SIX   Place the LED sequins behind their holes, so that the centers poke through the front face. Tape down any slack thread, making sure that no piece of thread overlaps or touches any other—be sure to pay special attention to where the folds are made; if the threads touch each other it will cause a short circuit and the LED lights won't work anymore.

STEP SEVEN   Glue the top corners together to hide the circuit behind the flaps.

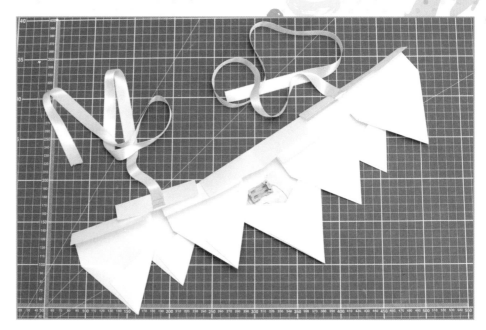

STEP EIGHT Lay all seven pieces together, as shown here. The large piece with the lights should be placed in the center.

STEP NINE Glue the pieces together, starting at the center and working outward. Leave the flap of the last piece on the right unglued. This is important because the end of the left side will be inserted to form the circular shape. Let the glue dry

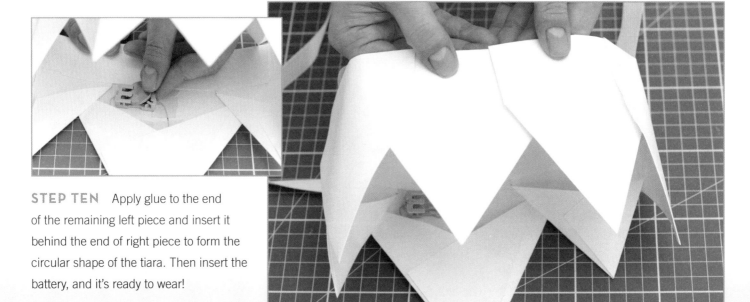

STEP TEN Apply glue to the end of the remaining left piece and insert it behind the end of right piece to form the circular shape of the tiara. Then insert the battery, and it's ready to wear!

MINIATURE ORIGAMI

WITH STACIE TAMAKI

MINIATURE BOX

MINIATURE LILY

MINIATURE CRANE

MINIATURE BOX

A traditional origami box is an easy model to begin with, whether you're a novice folder or an experienced folder learning to fold in miniature. Note that it is imperative to reduce the size of one square of paper if your goal is to fold a two-piece lidded box.

MATERIALS
- Glue stick
- For a small box (1" x 1" by 0.5" high):
  1 piece of 3" x 3" paper (lid) and 1 piece of 2.75" x 2.75" (bottom)
- For a tiny box (0.5" x 0.5" by 0.25" high):
  1 piece of 1.5" x 1.5" paper (lid) and 1 piece of 1.625" x 1.625" paper (bottom)

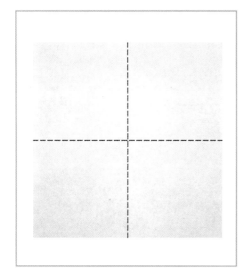

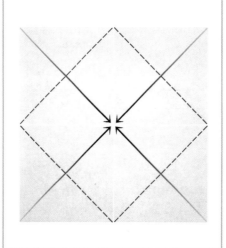

STEP ONE Lay the paper for the box bottom color-side down. Fold in half from top to bottom. Set the fold with your fingernail or a folding stick. Unfold, and fold in half from left to right. Unfold again. The paper should be divided into four equal sections.

STEP TWO Now fold each of the four outer corners toward the center, using the fold lines as a guide to keep things squared as you fold.

STEP THREE Your model should now look like this. The flaps may not lay perfectly flat, but as long as they are folded evenly that's okay.

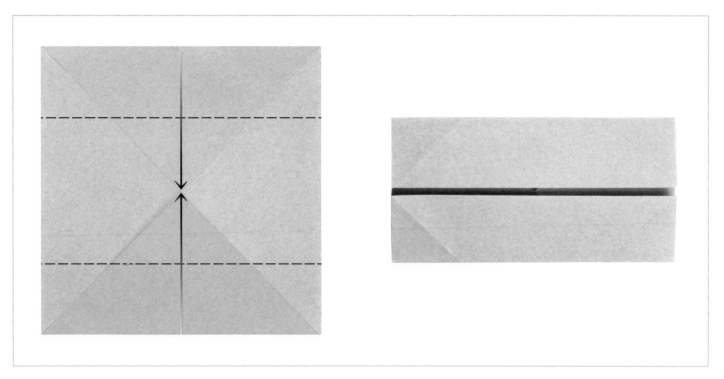

STEP FOUR   Now fold the upper and lower edges towards the center. Crease well along each fold, and then unfold.

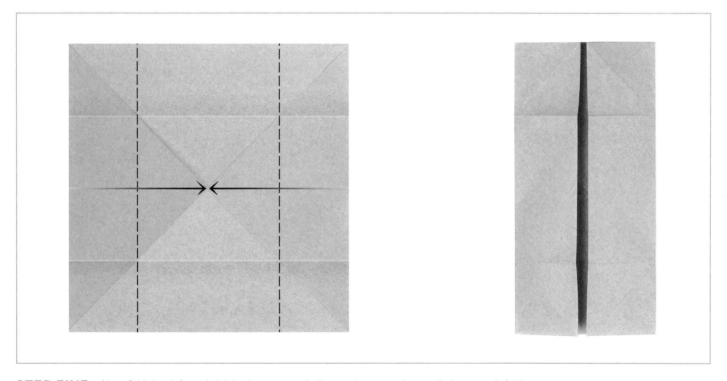

STEP FIVE   Now fold the left and right edges towards the center, creasing well along each fold.

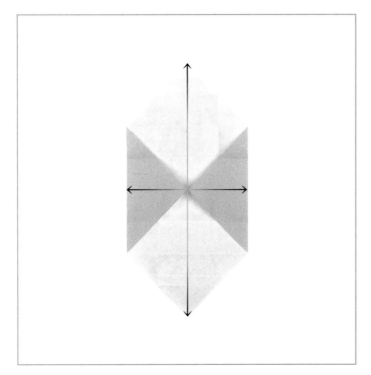

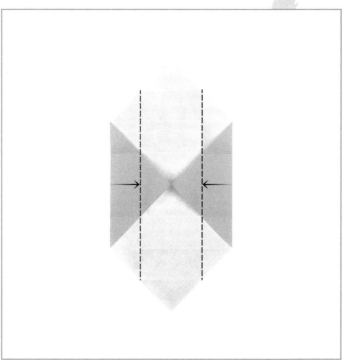

STEP SIX Unfold the left and right sections, and then unfold the top and bottom sections, opening them up as pictured.

STEP SEVEN Refold the left and right edges upward to form two sides of the box. There will already be guideline creases in place from step five.

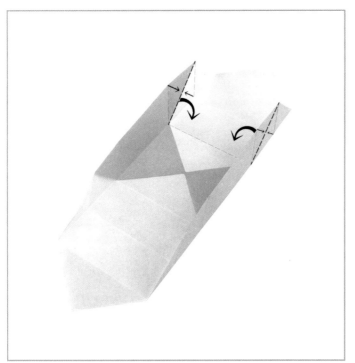

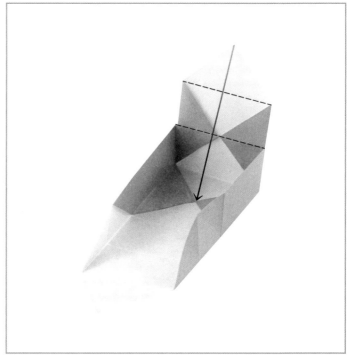

STEP EIGHT Using the dotted lines and arrows in the diagram, find the diagonal creases and guide them toward each other so that each side folds inward upon itself. Next fold downward along each of the two dotted lines by bringing the top point of the paper to the center of the box.

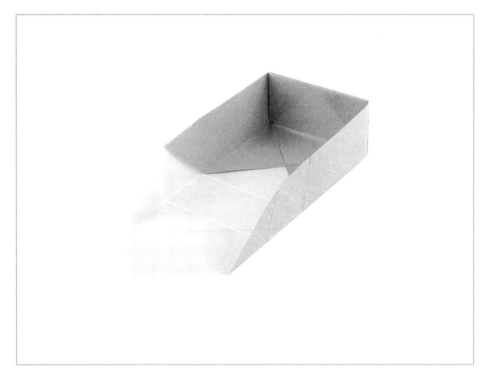

STEP NINE The box will look like this once the fold is completed. Now repeat this step on the other unfinished side.

STEP TEN Repeat using the second square of paper (which should be slightly larger or smaller, depending on which sheet you began with) to create the other half of your lidded box.

MINIATURE LILY

While there are other more complicated water lily patterns, this one works best for working in miniature. One piece of paper forms a traditional water lily model. Three in graduated sizes (held in place by a little glue) creates a fancier model that is easily within the realm of possibilities.

MATERIALS
- White craft glue
- For a small flower (1" x 1" by 0.75" high):
  1 piece of 3" x 3" paper (outer petals), 1 piece of 2.5" x 2.5" paper (middle petals), and 1 piece of 1.5" x 1.5" yellow paper (inner petals)
- For a tiny flower (0.5" x 0.5" by 0.3" high):
  1 piece of 1.5" x 1.5" paper (outer petals), 1 piece of 1.125" x 1.125" paper (middle petals), and 1 piece of 0.75" x 0.75" yellow paper (inner petals)

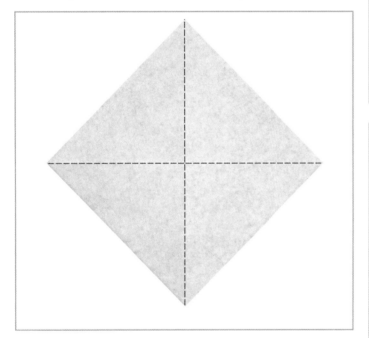

STEP ONE Start with the paper color-side down. Fold in half from top to bottom, and set the fold with your fingernail or a folding stick. Unfold, and fold in half from left to right. Unfold again. The paper should be divided into four equal sections.

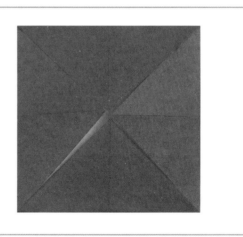

STEP TWO Fold each outer corner to the center of the paper. The flaps may not lay perfectly flat. That's okay as long as they are squared, as shown in step three.

TIP

YOU CAN USE SOLID OR PATTERNED PAPERS. I LIKE TO USE TWO COMPLEMENTING PAPERS THAT ARE SIMILAR COLORS BUT DIFFERENT IN PATTERN FOR THE OUTER AND MIDDLE PETALS AND BRIGHT YELLOW FOR THE INNER PETALS.

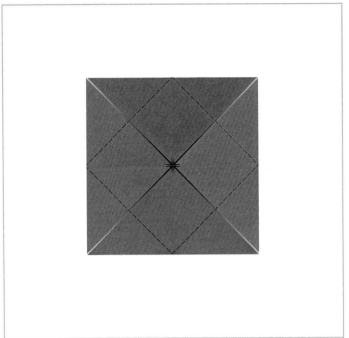

STEP THREE   Now fold along each of the four dotted lines by bringing each outer corner inward to meet in the center.

STEP FOUR   Your model should look like this. Flip the model over, and repeat the same steps to fold all four outer corners inward to the center of the model.

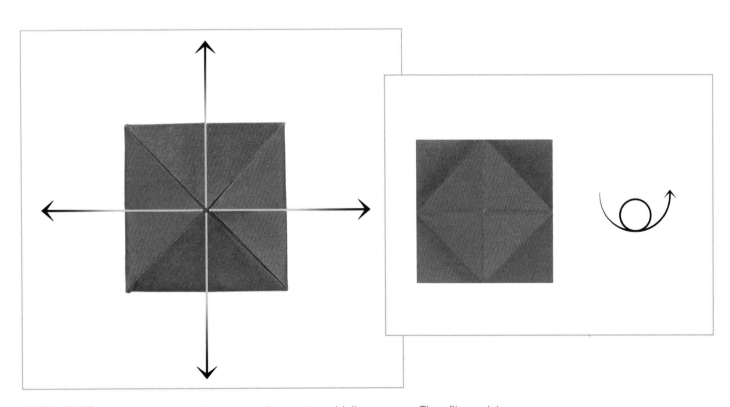

STEP FIVE   Unfold all four sections outward to create guideline creases. Then flip model over.

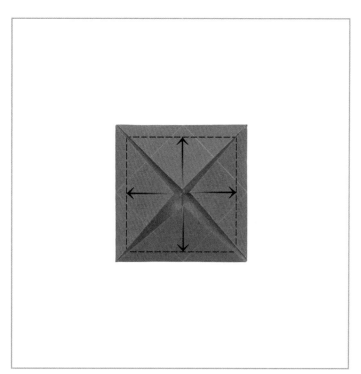
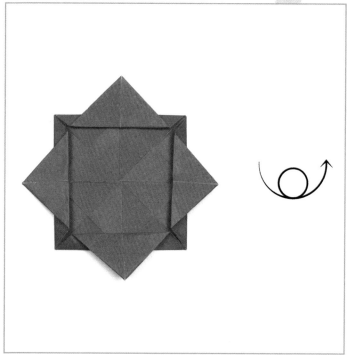

STEP SIX   Fold each section outward along the dotted lines, leaving some paper in place along the outer edge. For a small lily, I leave approximately ⅛" (inner petals) to ³⁄₁₆" (outer petals) between the dotted line and the outer edge. For a tiny lily, I leave approximately ¹⁄₁₆" (inner petals) to ⅛" (outer petals) between the dotted lines and the outer edge. You may find tweezers helpful when folding this step for a tiny lily. Flip the model over.

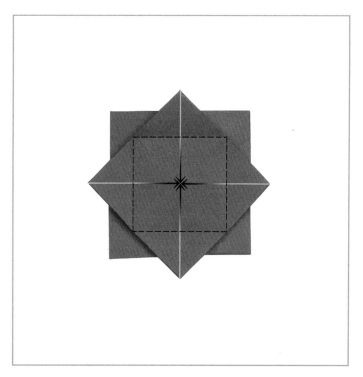

STEP SEVEN   Fold all four outer corners of the top level of paper toward the center. I like to dab a glue stick in the central area before folding the corners in to help hold things in place. These four folds will create the four upright petals that comprise the flower.

STEP EIGHT   Note that there are two layers of petals—a short interior set and a taller exterior petal nested together. Before following the arrows in the image use your fingernail or the wide end of a bamboo skewer, round chopstick, or wooden dowel to gently push the interior petals together until they meet and form a point. Now gently pinch the bottom half of the petals where the black arrows are. I brace the underside of the petal against my index finger and push down toward it very gently with my thumb to make the tip of each petal point in a more inward/downward direction.

STEP NINE   Next make two more flowers in graduating sizes. Keep the largest outer set of petals flat at the bottom. For the two interior sets, pinch together slightly so they are more cupped.

TIP

TO ADD YOUR WATER LILY TO AN ORIGAMI BOX, SIMPLY ADD AN ADDITIONAL DAB OF WHITE CRAFT GLUE TO THE BOTTOM OF THE FLOWER AND CENTER IT ON THE LID OF THE BOX. IT'S THAT EASY! THE FLOWER CAN BE A GIFT ITSELF OR—MY FAVORITE USE—AN ORNAMENT ON A GIFT BOX IN PLACE OF A BOW.

STEP TEN   Place a dab of white craft glue on the bottom center of the smallest lily. Using your fingers or tweezers, place the small flower in the medium flower—you can also use a toothpick to gently guide the petals into place. I like to rotate each flower 90 degrees so that their petals are never aligned—this makes the finished flower fuller in appearance. Apply a slight amount of pressure for about 10-20 seconds as the glue dries. Repeat to glue the medium lily into the larger petals.

MINIATURE CRANE

The origami crane is the most recognizable and beloved of all the Japanese paper folds. Folding 1000 paper cranes is symbolic of world peace, good luck, and a long life.

MATERIALS

- For a small crane (0.75" high): 1 square of 1.5" paper
- For a tiny crane (0.375" high): 1 square of 0.75" paper

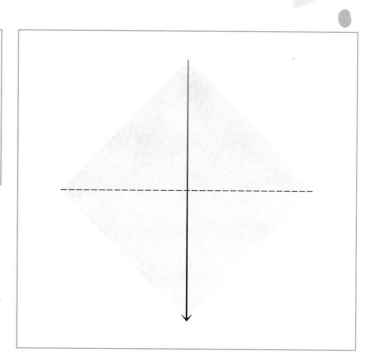

STEP ONE   Lay the paper color-side down. Fold in half from top to bottom along the dotted line. Set the fold with your fingernail or a folding stick.

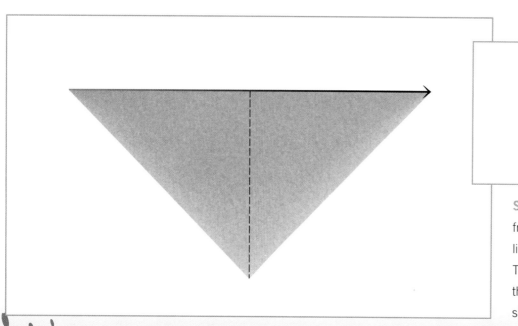

STEP TWO   Fold in half again from left to right along the dotted line. Don't forget to set the fold! The paper should be folded on the left side, and the top and right sides split apart.

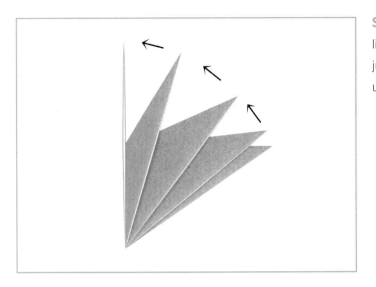

STEP THREE Now lift the top section you just folded over, and unfold it halfway.

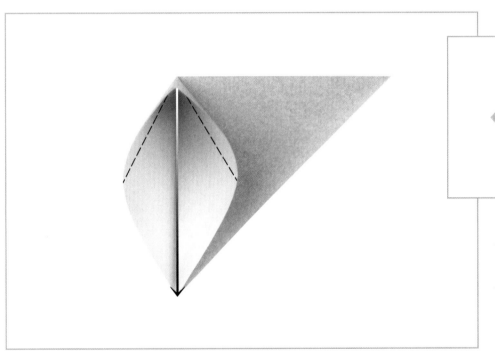

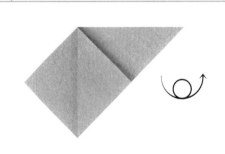

STEP FOUR Open the section and fold it flat by bringing the top center and bottom center points together until they meet, forming a square.

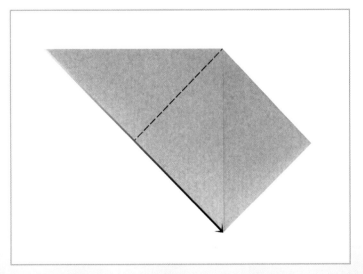

STEP FIVE Flip the paper over. To replicate the same fold on the other side you'll need to first create a guideline crease. Do this by bringing the far point on the left down to the center point at the base of the model, and fold the paper along the dotted line. Unfold, and open the section and use the guideline crease to fold the left point to the bottom point, replicating the square shape you just made in step four.

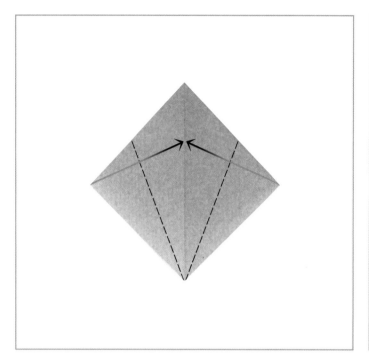

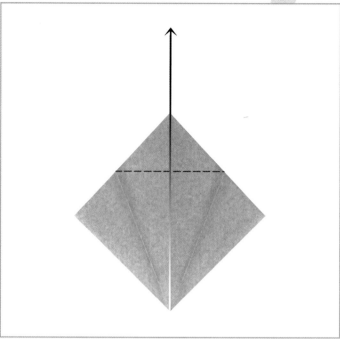

STEP SIX One side at a time, fold along the dotted lines to create new guideline folds. Bring the side points on each side to the center line, which will bring the entire lower edge to the center along with them. After creating the guideline creases unfold both sides.

STEP SEVEN This is the trickiest part. Note where the guideline creases begin toward the top of the model. Take the top section of the model, and raise and lift it upwards, folding it along the dotted line where the guideline creases begin. Be sure to fold only up to the interior edges—or even just a hair short of them—and not beyond.

STEP EIGHT As you do so, the model will begin to fold on the guideline creases (both above and below the center line). You may need to give a nudge or a pull here or there to straighten things out a bit more.

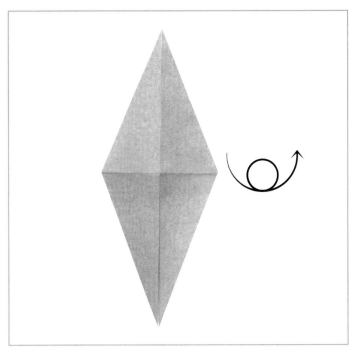

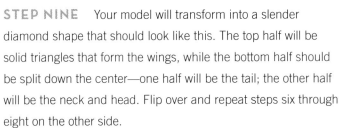

STEP NINE Your model will transform into a slender diamond shape that should look like this. The top half will be solid triangles that form the wings, while the bottom half should be split down the center—one half will be the tail; the other half will be the neck and head. Flip over and repeat steps six through eight on the other side.

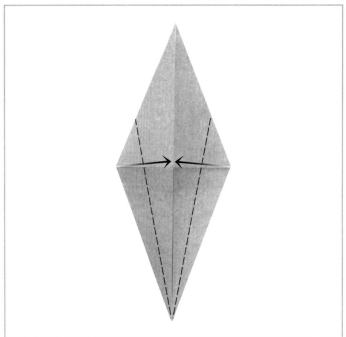

STEP TEN Make sure the upper half of the model is the solid half and the lower half is split down the middle. One side at a time, fold along the dotted lines by bringing each outer corner up to (but not extending beyond) the center line. Flip and repeat on the other side.

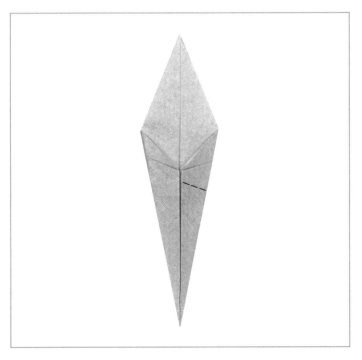

STEP ELEVEN The next step is to fold the neck and tail upwards. The dotted line indicates where the fold should take place. To create the fold you will open and flatten the neck.

STEP TWELVE Open and flatten the neck. Follow both sets of arrows to simultaneously pinch the neck shut along the dotted center line while also rotating the neck upward from the dotted line along the base.

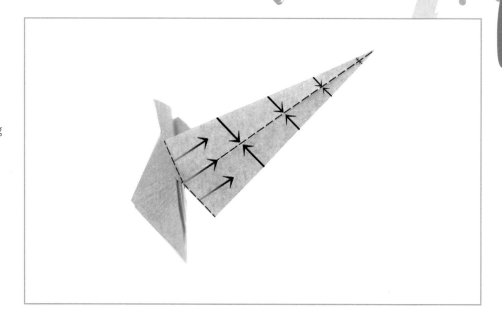

STEP THIRTEEN As you rotate and pinch the neck (or tail) shut, this image illustrates how the fold rotates into the upright position. You can decide if you want to make the neck and tail vertical or set them at an angle away from the body. You could stop the rotation at the second-to-last point or somewhere in between the last two positions. After folding both sides stop and assess them. The side that is more even and cleanly folded should be the tail. If one side is a bit wonky I choose that one as the neck/head.

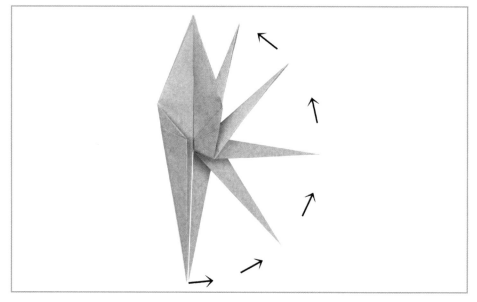

STEP FOURTEEN To fold the head, repeat the same technique, opening the end of the neck and flattening it as you fold it downward; allow it to close on itself to form the head. There is no "correct" size to make the head. Fold it as far up or down the neck as you'd like to—whatever is most appealing to you is the right size!

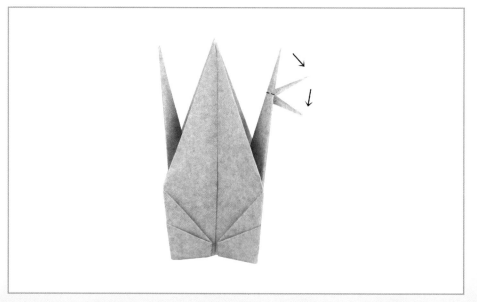

WET-FOLD ORIGAMI

WITH PAUL FRASCO

TREE

OWL

GNOME

GETTING STARTED

If you're a fan of paper folding, you've probably experienced watching your finished origami model immediately begin to sag and spread. You're not alone. Since the origin of origami, origamists have been fighting gravity with new and innovative techniques, including wires, glue, and foil-backed paper.

Over the last few decades, the best folders in the world have turned their knowledge of how paper is made to their advantage and added a new weapon to their arsenal—wet folding! Using the wet-folding technique helps your models stand the test of time and brings them to a whole new level of beauty.

What is wet folding? You've probably experienced it already without even knowing it. If you have ever accidentally put a worn dollar bill through the laundry and had it come out of the dryer feeling crisp and new, you have experienced wet folding. So, what happened to that dollar bill, and how can we use this concept to transform a classic origami crane into the beautiful swan shown above?

It turns out that paper is smarter than you know. In fact, it has a memory. When we wet fold, we use water to literally change the memory of the paper so that it "remembers" the final shape of the model. This allows us to add gentle curves and fine details, and it also provides added stability to the finished creation.

HOW DOES IT WORK?

Wet folding is exactly what it sounds like—the paper is folded when wet, so the fibers in the paper bend and stretch without breaking. As it dries, the fibers naturally remember the final position. Almost all papers can be wet folded, but the best results come when the paper you select has the right combination of two key ingredients in paper manufacturing: pulp and sizing.

SUPPLIES

For wet folding you'll need to gather a few common household supplies.

Paper Towels   I use a lot of paper towels when wet folding, because they are my preferred method of applying water to paper. You could also use spray bottles or specialty watercolor paintbrushes, both of which are good options.

Acrylic Paint   We'll talk more about paint a bit later. You could use other types of paint, but acrylic dries quickly and has good color saturation, which is what makes it my favorite.

Utility Knife   As you apply water to the paper and the fibers soak it up, the paper will expand. Some papers will expand quite a bit, requiring you to trim one edge of the paper with a utility knife to make it square and ready for folding.

A Self-healing Cutting Mat   These are great for all types of art projects, and I couldn't live without mine! This isn't a required tool, but it is highly recommended.

PICKING THE PERFECT PAPER

In order to choose the perfect paper, it's important to know more about paper basics. Paper is comprised of many elements, but there are two that are important to consider: pulp and sizing.

PULP   If you have been unsuccessful in your origami attempts because the paper keeps splitting, ripping, or tearing, it's the pulp. Every piece of paper is made from pulp, and the most common kind is wood pulp. Most paper around the home or office is made primarily of wood pulp. These papers are relatively brittle and tear easily, due to the very short fibers. This makes them suitable for practice but not very good for finished display models.

You want to use paper that has long, natural fibers, which are less likely to break. It's also good to use paper that has a high degree of some other long, natural fiber, such as cotton, cotton rag, or mulberry. Longer fibers make for a tighter weave, and the paper is more resistant to splitting. My personal favorite paper is made from 66% cotton rag. Look for papers labeled as cotton or rag papers at your local art & craft store.

SIZING   Sizing is added to paper to prevent ink from soaking into the pulp fibers. Without sizing ink would bleed into the paper, making the printing smudged and blotchy. But sizing does something else that is important for wet-fold origami. Sizing is the key to the paper's memory. It is the glue holding the pulp fibers together. It makes the paper ridged and allows it to retain its flat surface. When we wet fold, the sizing helps the paper remember its new shape. Common sizing components include resin and starch, but my favorite paper is made with gelatin sizing.

Some paper has very little or no sizing at all. This paper will be limp and won't retain its shape well. Imagine trying to fold a cloth napkin or t-shirt. If the paper you want to use is limp and shapeless, don't worry—you can add your own sizing! (See page 118 for details.)

THE BASICS OF WET FOLDING

Begin each wet-folding project by wetting the paper. In each of the projects that follow, I apply water evenly over the entire sheet of paper before I start folding. By wetting the entire sheet, the finished model will have a soft organic look. All you need is a glass or jar of water and some paper towels. Fold a paper towel in half several times to create a small pad, and use it to apply water to the paper. Shown at left, I apply water to a piece of tree bark-patterned paper to begin an origami tree.

If you want a crisper look for your finished model that looks similar to traditional origami, use the paper towel pad to apply water only to the area you are folding as you make each fold. This is a great technique that was taught to me by origami master Michael LaFosse and can produce amazing effects!

The key to wet folding is to have a good sense for how wet the paper should be. You want it to be moist, but not damp. If the paper is too dry, you will feel the "crispness" when you fold it; if it is too wet, the fibers will start to pull apart or get "fuzzy." With the right amount of wetness, the paper retains some tension but will also give. I recommend testing a small piece of your paper by folding a classic crane before attempting more intricate models. This will allow you to get a feel for the paper and avoid frustration.

PREPARING PAPER FOR FOLDING

Finding the perfect piece of paper can be a challenge. You may find a great pattern, but the paper composition is not quite right, or you need a duo-color paper that you can't find. Most stores have a limited selection of paper types and patterns, and there may not be a specialty story near you. As an artist, I have tackled this problem in a variety of ways. I have glued multiple sheets together, I have special ordered paper online, and I have even tried making my own paper from scratch. I tried all of these options before realizing I should take what I have and turn it into the perfect sheet.

Add Your Own Sizing

If you want to use a sheet of handmade or specialty paper, you likely need to add sizing to make it suitable for wet folding. The most readily available sizing is methylcellulose (MC), a water-soluble glue available in the framing section of most craft stores. It come as both a powder and a liquid and is sometimes also referred to as bookbinding glue. If you purchase the powder, start by mixing it with water and letting it dissolve—follow the directions on the package, and remember that you can always add more water or powder if the consistency isn't right at first. Use a foam brush to apply the sizing to the paper.

PAINT & COLOR THEORY

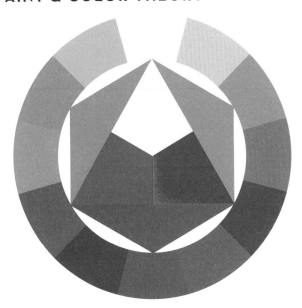

When selecting your paint colors, there are a couple key concepts to remember. There are three primary colors: red, yellow, and blue. These colors, when mixed in different proportions, create all the other colors of the rainbow. This concept can be visualized with the color wheel. Between each of the primary colors are the secondary and tertiary colors, which result from mixing the primary colors. For example, mixing yellow and blue makes green. Colors on opposite sides of the wheel are complementary colors. While they complement each other individually in a painting, mixing them as a base color will create a muddy mess. Stick with colors that are close together on the color wheel to create harmonious and rich color schemes for your projects.

Painting Your Own Paper

Hardly anything in nature is one single, solid color. To get the best look for a finished model, build up the color by applying a base color and then adding a highlight or lowlight. I prefer to work from a dark base, and then apply highlights, which gives the paper a more earth-weathered look. If you start with a light color, the result will be a brighter or more luminous finished product. The choice is yours—just remember that variation in color will give your finished models a more natural look. When applying paint to a large area you can use a large foam brush or paper towel. Painting your own paper is the perfect way to add texture and a touch of realism to your origami projects. Use the technique demonstrated below to create bark and feather texture.

Painting Bark or Feathers

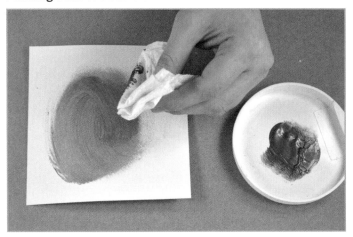

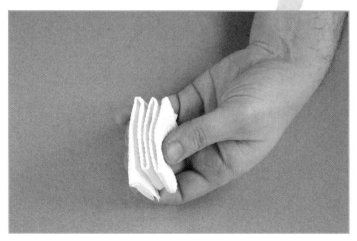

Start by applying a base coat of paint to the paper. To make a spotted owl pattern, I apply a base of gray or silver across the entire sheet, as shown above. For a tree, use a base coat of burnt umber or burnt sienna.

Fold a paper towel in half lengthwise several times, and then in half several times to create a small pad with multiple thick layers, as shown. To create feather texture, make each layer shorter than the previous. To create bark texture, make longer layers or add rolls in the layers to achieve a knotted look.

Now use the paper towel like a stamp to apply bark or feather texture to the paper. Stamp lightly so that the paper towel layers don't clump together. It's a good idea to use a piece of scrap paper to stamp first to remove excess paint. Use these techniques to paint your own papers for the tree and owl origami projects on pages 122-133.

Painting Multi-color Patterns

You can also apply multiple colors to the same sheet of paper. The key to this kind of paint application is to achieve a clean line between each of the colors. Follow these steps to paint your own paper for the gnome origami project on pages 134-143.

Start by marking the paper in quarters along the edge with a pencil or a small pinch.

Next tape off one section of the paper.

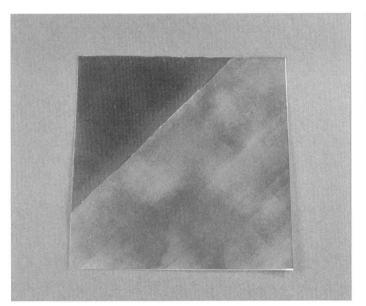

Apply the first paint color to one of the sections of the paper. Let the paint dry, and then gently remove the tape. Realign the tape along the edge of the paint, and apply the second paint color.

For the gnome origami project, flip the paper over and tape off about two-thirds of the paper. Paint the larger section pink.

TREE

DESIGN BY PAUL FRASCO

This origami tree is formed from a common base called the bird base. It's a bit ironic that this tree starts with a bird base and the owl on pages 128-133 begins from another base altogether! Wet the paper before you begin, or wet each fold as you work.

STEP ONE   Begin with the bark side facing up. Valley-fold the paper in half diagonally, and then unfold.

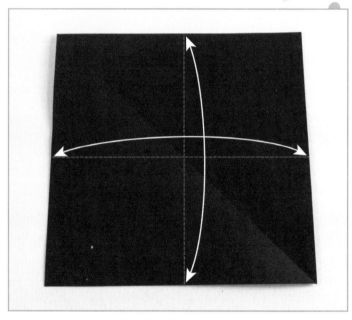

STEP TWO   Valley-fold the paper from edge to edge.

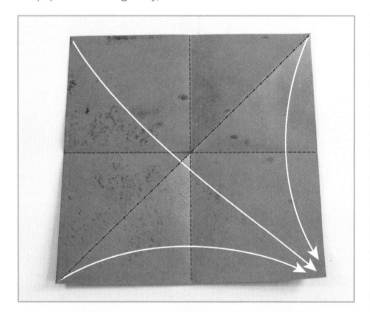

STEP THREE   Flip the paper over, and then bring the four corners together using the existing creases.

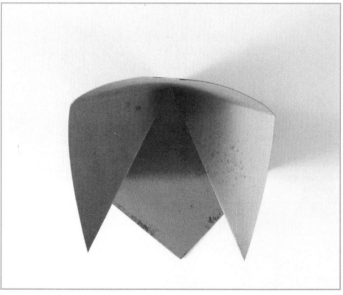

STEP FOUR Divide the top layer in quarters, and then valley-fold the edge to the center line. Repeat with the new edge until you have created quarters, for a total of six folds.

STEP FIVE Crimp the innermost creases that you created in step four.

STEP SIX Inside reverse-fold the remaining quarter.

STEP SEVEN Repeat on the other side.

STEP EIGHT Repeat steps four through seven on the back.

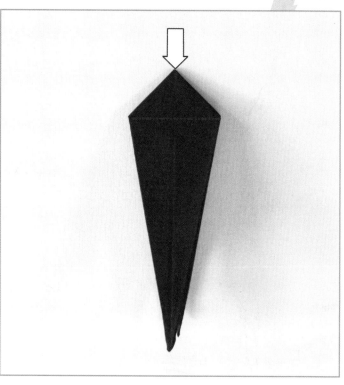

STEP NINE Sink the top corner of the model into the point so that it is flat across the top.

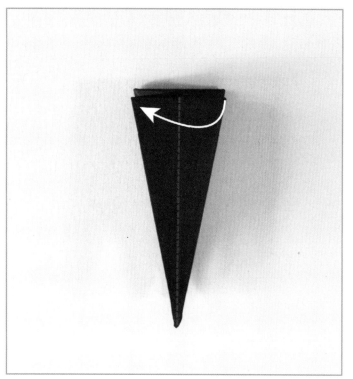

STEP TEN Then valley-fold the model in half along the center line.

STEP ELEVEN Inside-reverse fold each of the hidden corners.

STEP TWELVE   Valley-fold the outer layer.

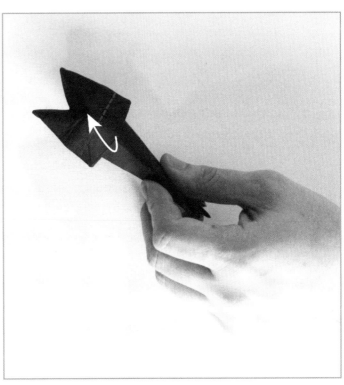

STEP THIRTEEN   Valley-fold the flap in half.

STEP FOURTEEN   Inside-reverse fold the newly created corners to form roots. Rotate the model 180 degrees to the branch's face.

STEP FIFTEEN   Outside-reverse fold the outermost branch.

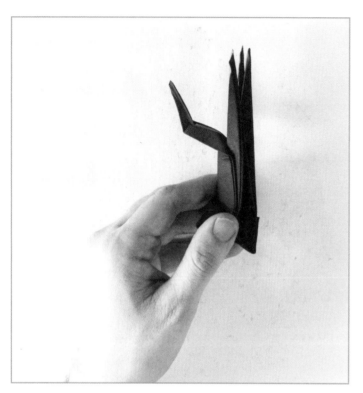

STEP SIXTEEN   Crimp the end of the branch.

STEP SEVENTEEN   Inside-reverse fold the innermost branch.

STEP EIGHTEEN   Inside-reverse fold the end of one of the inner branches.

STEP NINETEEN   Twist the branches to expose the inner layers and create barklike texture.

STEP TWENTY Wrap the tree around the center with a piece of paper towel and set upright to dry. While the paper dries, press the roots flat to create a good base for the tree.

STEP TWENTY-ONE Once dry, remove the paper towel, and the tree is complete!

O W L

DESIGN BY PAUL FRASCO

Once you've mastered the origami tree, make some owls to add to your origami forest. This is a fun and fresh take on the more traditional crane and swan models.

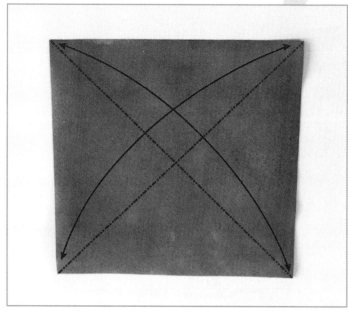

STEP ONE   Prep your paper with a light wash of water, using a paper towel.

STEP TWO   Valley-fold the paper from corner to corner on both sides.

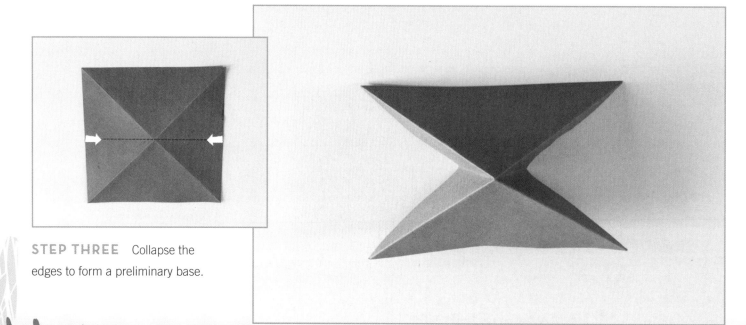

STEP THREE   Collapse the edges to form a preliminary base.

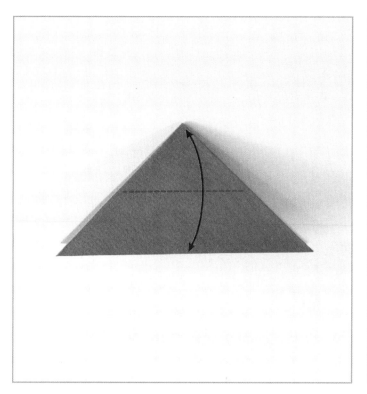

STEP FOUR Mountain-fold in half, and then unfold.

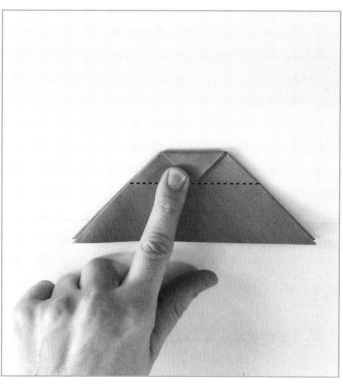

STEP FIVE Now mountain-fold the tip to the crease you made in the previous step.

STEP SIX Next mountain-fold the wings inward, parallel to the top of the head. Fold only the top layer of paper.

STEP SEVEN Mountain-fold the tip of the top triangle up to form the beak.

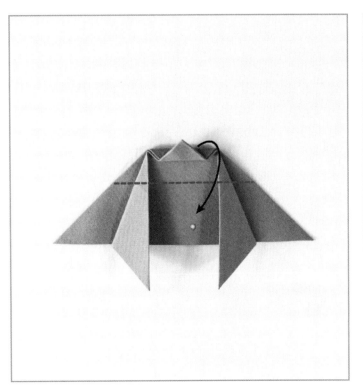 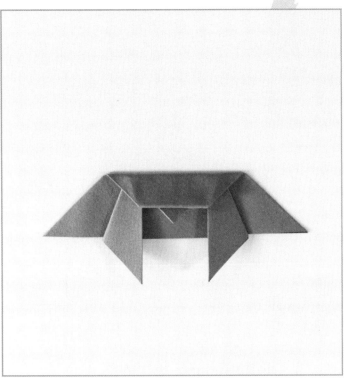

STEP EIGHT   Mountain-fold the top of the head down, using the existing creases.

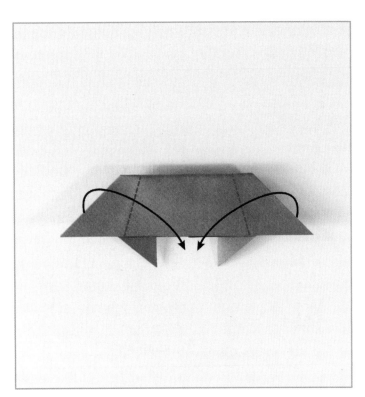 

STEP NINE   Flip the piece over. Mountain-fold the flaps inward to form the claws of the owl.

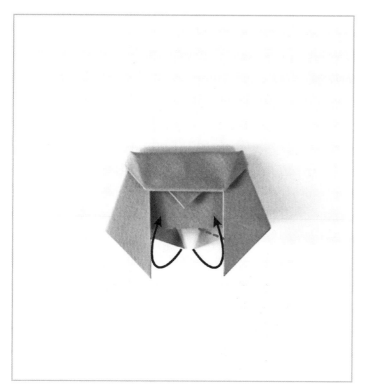

STEP TEN   Flip the piece over again. Mountain-fold the claws up.

STEP ELEVEN   Next fold the tips of the claws down.

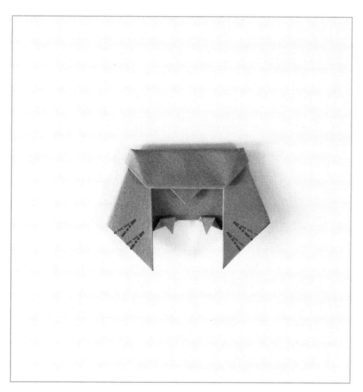

STEP TWELVE   Crimp the wings as shown here to make the model three-dimensional.

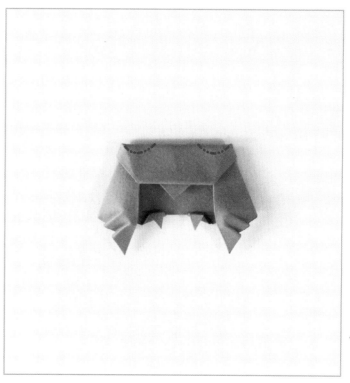

STEP THIRTEEN   Crimp the sides to finish rounding the model, and then create small horns.

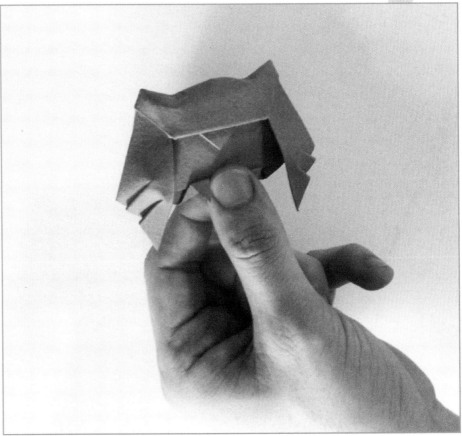

STEP FOURTEEN

The finished crimp will make the top of the head round and create a hollow cavity in the back of the model.

STEP FIFTEEN

Wrap the model with a paper towel to hold its shape, and set it aside to dry.

STEP SIXTEEN   Once dry, place the finished owl in the tree for a perfect perch.

GNOME

DESIGN BY PAUL FRASCO

Add a little whimsy to your origami forest with a quirky gnome. Use the tips and instruction on pages 119-121 to paint your own paper!

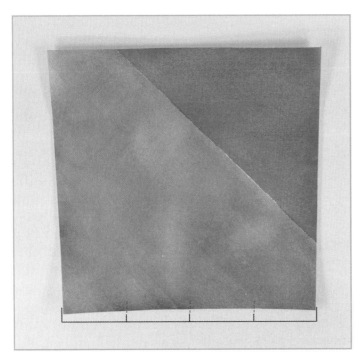

STEP ONE   Mark the paper in quarters along one edge, with a pinch at each quarter. (See step two.)

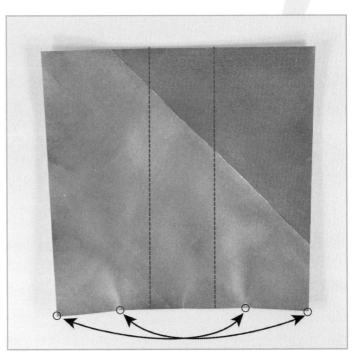

STEP TWO   Valley-fold each edge to the opposite quarter marked in step one. Then unfold.

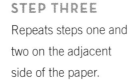

STEP THREE
Repeats steps one and two on the adjacent side of the paper.

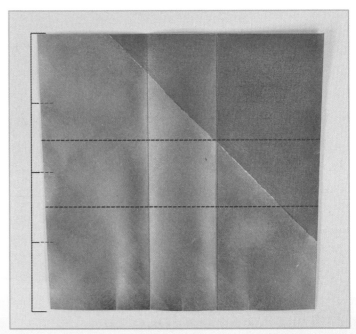

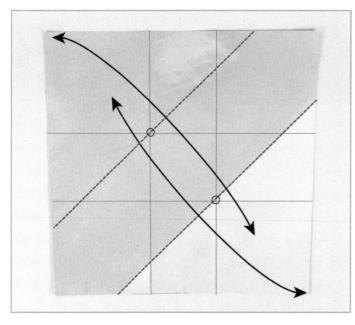

STEP FOUR Flip the paper over, and valley-fold diagonally, using the intersection of existing creases as a guide. The creases should line up with the edge of the paint colors on both sides. Unfold.

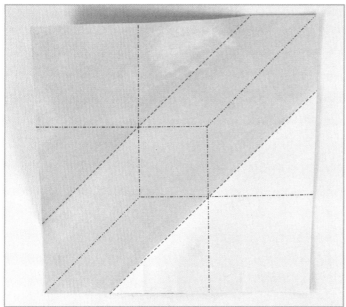

STEP FIVE Collapse the sheet using the existing creases. Valley-fold across the center to make the model lie flat. See the dotted red line in the image above right for where the fold should go.

STEP SIX The model should look like this after the collapse.

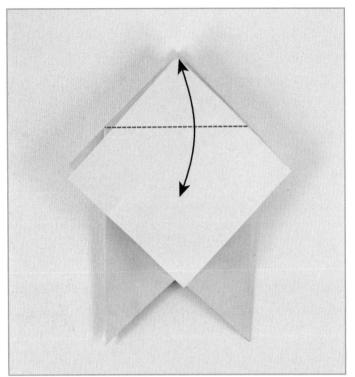

STEP SEVEN Valley-fold the top layer, and then unfold.

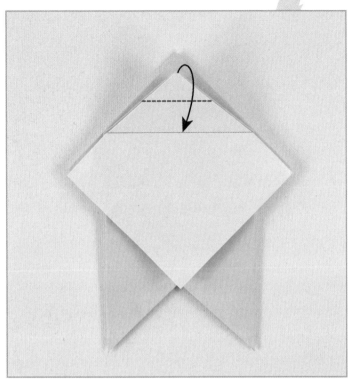

STEP EIGHT Next valley-fold just the tip to the newly created crease line.

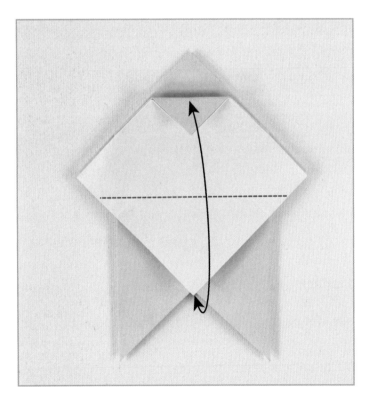

STEP NINE Valley-fold the top layer to the tip of the nose, and then unfold.

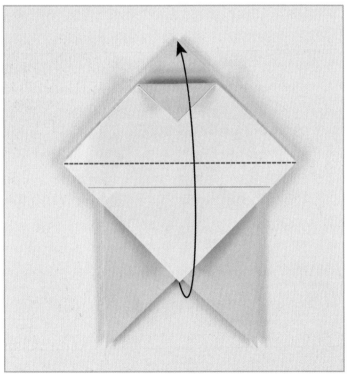

STEP TEN Valley-fold the top flap in half.

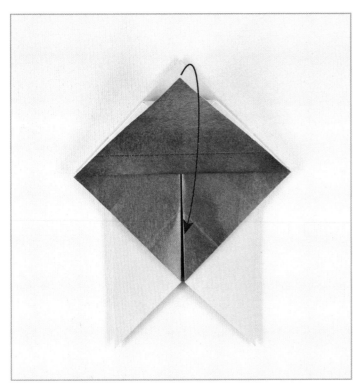

STEP ELEVEN Reverse the existing crease that you created in step ten.

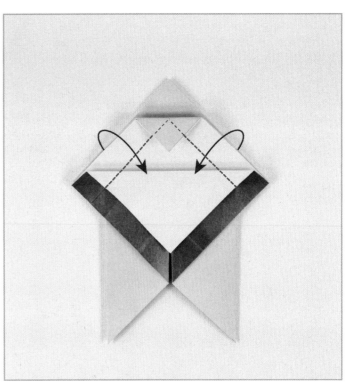

STEP TWELVE Valley-fold the top flaps inward to lock the nose in place.

STEP THIRTEEN Mountain-fold the flaps behind.

STEP FOURTEEN Sink the top point into the head.

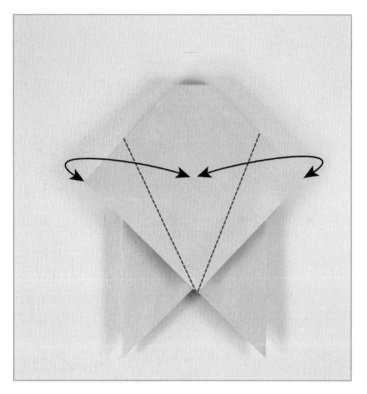

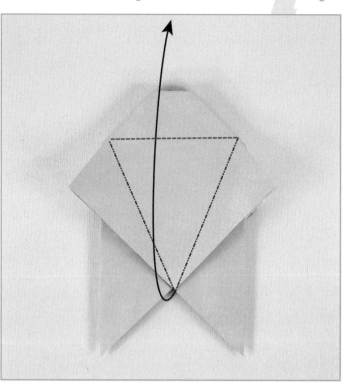

STEP FIFTEEN   Turn the model over, and valley-fold the corners to the center. Then unfold.

STEP SIXTEEN   Petal-fold the head, using the creases from the previous step as a guide.

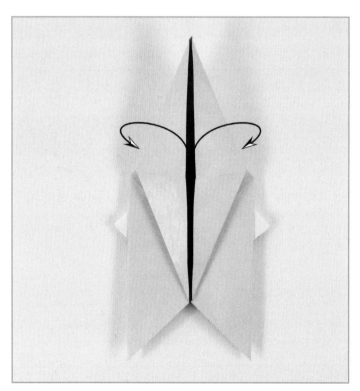

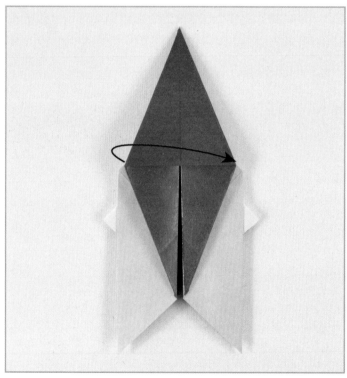

STEP SEVENTEEN   Unwrap, and reverse the flaps to change the color. (See step eighteen.)

STEP EIGHTEEN   Turn the left flap to expose the flaps beneath.

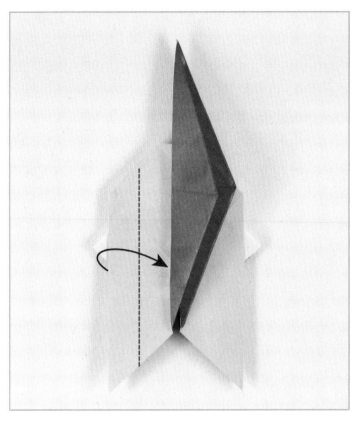

Valley-fold the leg flap
in half.

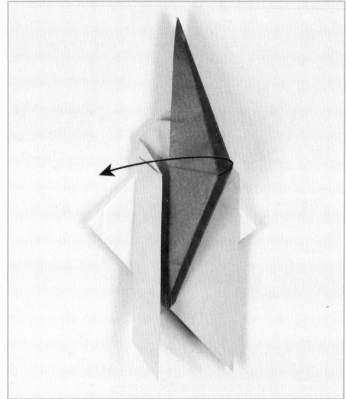

STEP TWENTY   Return the top flap to its previous position.

STEP TWENTY-ONE   Repeat steps eighteen through
twenty on the opposite side.

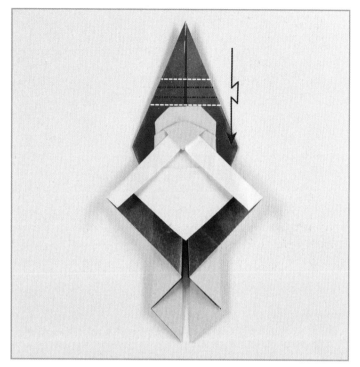 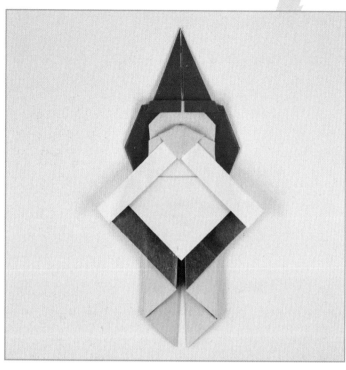

STEP TWENTY-TWO Turn over the model, and pleat the hat where it meets the head to make the brim of the hat.

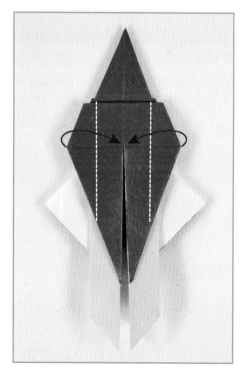 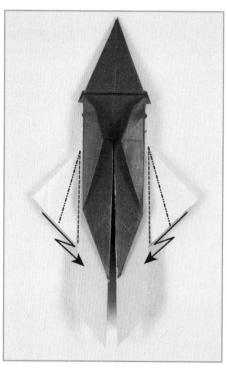

STEP TWENTY-THREE Turn over the model, and valley-fold the flaps to the center.

STEP TWENTY-FOUR Pleat as shown above to form the arms.

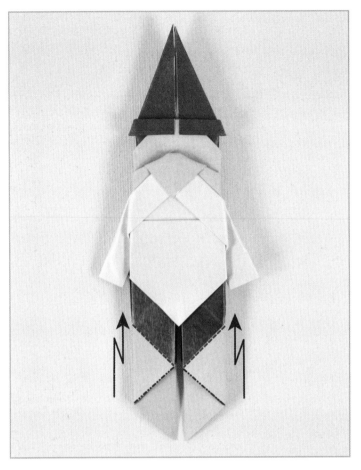

STEP TWENTY-FIVE   Turn the model over again, and pleat to form the feet.

STEP TWENTY-SIX   Pinch the white paper to form the beard.

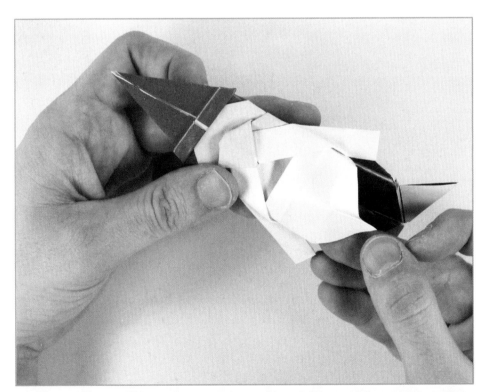

STEP TWENTY-SEVEN
Squeeze the model to make it three-dimensional.

STEP TWENTY-EIGHT
Pinch the hat to give it a crumpled look.

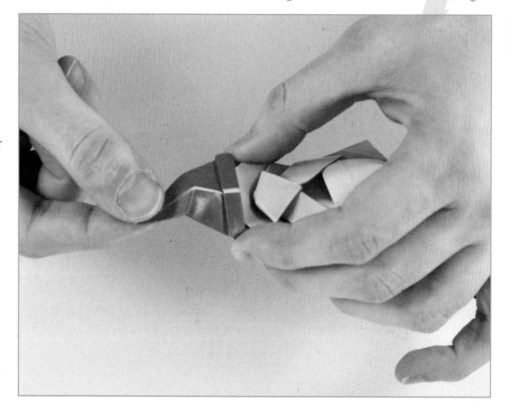

STEP TWENTY-NINE
Wrap the model or use clamps to hold the folds in place while it dries.

STEP THIRTY Once dry, remove the clips or paper towel pieces.

ABOUT THE AUTHORS

JENNY W. CHAN is an origami teacher, artist, and designer based in New York City. Her work has been featured on *Good Housekeeping*, Post-it® Brand, and more. She has been a guest speaker at Stream Con NYC and is also the first-place winner of The Craftys in the papercrafts and scrapbook category, which celebrates the best in crafts and DIY and is judged on technical expertise, creative expression, and innovation. Jenny is a YouTube™ NextUp winner, and offers free craft tutorials on her channel, home to over 10 million viewers and a rapidly growing fan base. Visit www.youtube.com/origamitree or www.origamitree.com to learn more.

PAUL FRASCO is an American origami designer focused on representational and animal designs. In his work, accurate proportions take a back seat to bringing emotion to the final design and creating a fun and accessible folding sequence. Paul's work has been featured in public spaces, museums, and galleries around the country. He has created models for such clients as the American Museum of Natural History and Stony Brook University. Visit www.wetfold.com to learn more.

COCO SATO is a UK-based Japanese artist, author, and speaker whose practice reinvents origami in uniquely modern ways. Coco combines art and technology in playful and simple ways, providing an accessible and fun gateway into electronics and programming to women and young girls. She is a winner of PANTONE® Color Inspires award and contributes to design blogs such as Design Sponge and Design Love Fest. Her conceptual piece, Roborigami, an interactive giant robotic origami installation that transforms public spaces into a playful Zen garden, has been featured in Design Milk and Creative Boom, as well as museums and international festivals. Visit www.cocosato.co.uk to learn more.

STACIE TAMAKI is an origami artist, lifestyle and travel blogger, photographer, and nature lover. She loves the art of paper folding because it was her maternal grandmother who taught her how to fold a paper crane when she was a small child. She resides in Western Michigan and enjoys traveling nationwide in her tiny glamper (glamorous + camper), aptly named "The Glampette." Stacie launched Tinygami, an art, lifestyle, and travel blog in 2015. She has been featured in *Tiny House Magazine*, the *TODAY Show*, HGTV's *Crafters Coast to Coast*, and on various new channels. Visit www.stacietamaki.com or www.tinygami.wordpress.com to learn more.

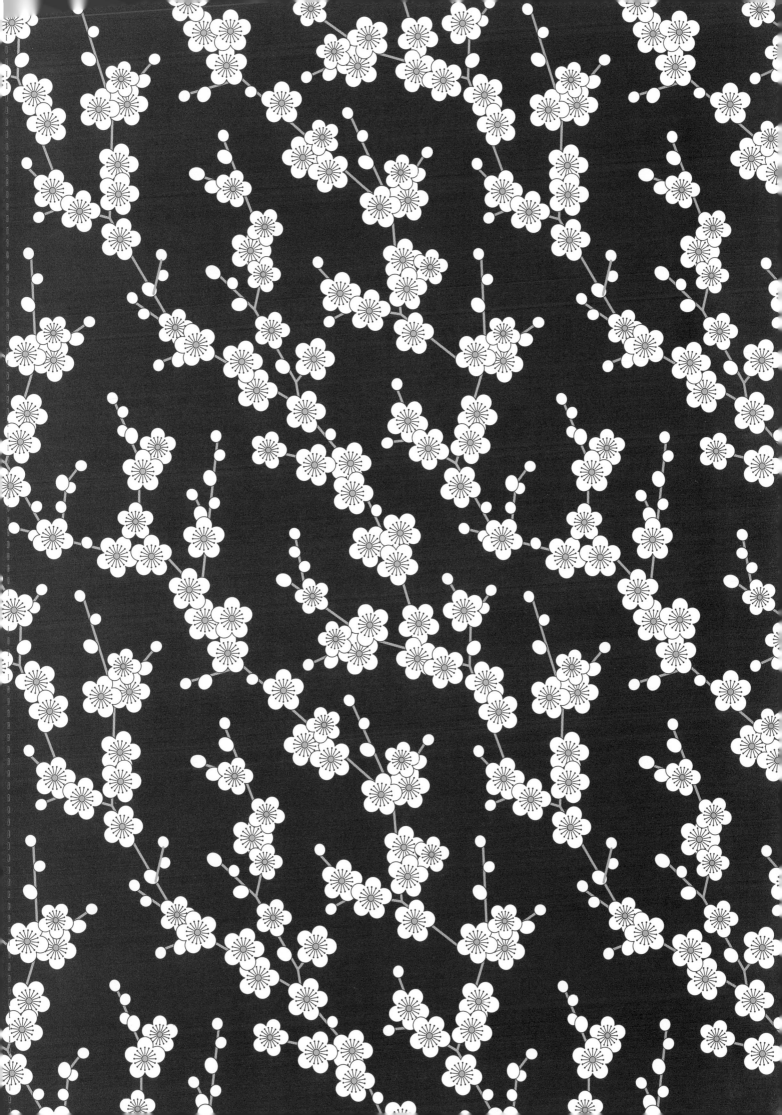

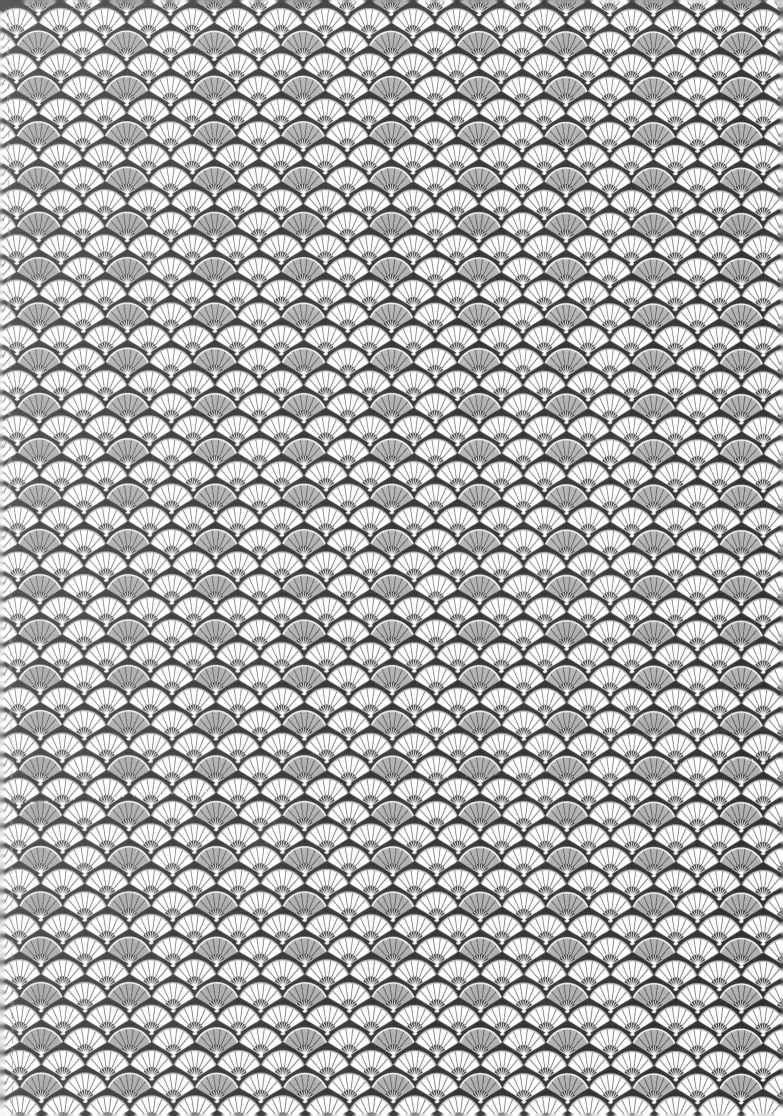